BRIDGE

FROM EAST TO WEST

CADEM

FLVVIVS

emms

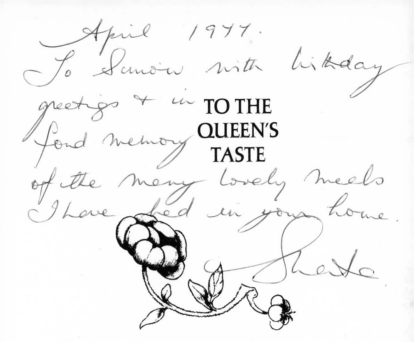

April 1977.

To Simon with birthday
greetings & in
fond memory
of the many lovely meals
I have fed in your home.

Sheila

TO THE QUEEN'S TASTE

COOK: Were you ever a cook?

POET: A Cook? no surely.

COOK: Then you can be no good poet: for a good
poet differs nothing at all from a master-cook.
Either's art is the wisdom of the mind.

BEN JONSON
Neptune's Triumph (1624)

ELISABETHA · D · G · ANGLIÆ · FRANCIÆ · ET · HIBERNIÆ · REGINA · FIDEI · DEFENSATRIX ·

TO THE QUEEN'S TASTE

Elizabethan feasts
and recipes adapted
for modern cooking

by Lorna J. Sass

**THE METROPOLITAN
MUSEUM OF ART**

LIBRARY OF CONGRESS CATALOGING IN PUBLICATION DATA

Sass, Lorna J.
  To the queen's taste.

  Bibliography: p.
  Includes index.
  1. Cookery, English.   I. Title.

TX717.S32   641.5'942   76-23242
ISBN 0-87099-151-5

FOR MY FRIENDS,
WHO KNOW
WHY

CONTENTS

PREFACE   11

INTRODUCTION   13

RECIPES

Appetizers

Rack of Veale on the French Fashion: 36
soup of veal simmered in wine with
turnips, carrots, and rosemary

Fartes of Portingale: 38
spicy lamb balls steamed in beef stock

Livering Puddinges: 40
liver-currant pâté with a hint of nutmeg

Baked Eeles: 42
eel, onions, and currants in a
covered pie

Herring Pye: 44
pickled herring and fruits baked in a
double crust

Entrées

Minst Pyes: 48
spicy mincemeat of ground veal, suet,
fruits, and rose water

Capon with Orenges After Mistres   50
Duffelds Way:
capon poached in spiced orange juice
and wine

Chickin Pie: 52
chicken baked with wine, dried fruits,
and spices

Piggs Petitoes: 54
pigs' feet cooked with wine and apples

Pudding in a Tench: 56
whole fish stuffed with spinach,
currants, and spices and baked in a
wine sauce

Quelquechose: 58
oyster-lamb casserole topped with
asparagus

Fresh Salmon: 60
salmon poached in beer with parsley,
thyme, and rosemary

Olive Pye: 62
veal scallops stuffed with spinach, violet
and strawberry leaves and baked in a
pie crust

Side Dishes

Artichoak Pye: 66
artichoke hearts baked with sherry,
dates, and orange peel

Lumbardy Tarts: 68
diced beets, currants, and cheese baked
in a pie

Pudding in a Turnep Root: 70
turnips stuffed with apples and currants
and steamed in wine

Tart of Beanes: 72
kidney beans and flavored cottage
cheese baked in a pie

Fritters of Spinnedge: 74
spinach-date balls dipped in ale batter
and fried

Quelquechose: 76
parsnips and marigolds cooked in
orange juice

Compound Sallet: 78
spinach and red cabbage dotted with
almonds, raisins, figs, capers, olives,
currants, pickles, and orange segments

Sauces

Sauce for a Gooce: 82
apples stewed in stock, vinegar, and
mustard

Sauce of Dry Proins: 84
prunes steeped in wine and cinnamon

Good Garlike Sauce: 85
garlic ground with almonds and
simmered in stock

Sauce for a Roast Capon: 86
onions cooked in wine and orange juice

Additions unto Sawces: 88
oranges boiled in wine and rose water

Desserts

Rice Puddings: 90
creamy rice pudding dotted with dates
and currants

Fine Cakes: 92
shortbread spiced with cloves and mace

Finer Jumbals: 94
almond cookies scented with rose water
and garnished with anise seeds

Course Ginger Bread: 96
sweet gingerbread with a hint of licorice

Tarte of Apples and Orenge Pilles: 98
apple and unpeeled orange slices
layered in a pie

A Warden Pie: 100
pear pie flavored with spices and rose
water

Tart of Almonds: 102
almond custard laced with rose water

Spinnage Tart: 104
sweetened spinach, wine, and rose water
in a pie

Miscellaneous

Of the Mixture of Paste: 108
pie pastry of butter, broth, and flour

To Make Paste Another Way: 110
pie pastry of butter, ale, egg, and flour

Another Way: 112
pie pastry scented with rose water

A Very Good Banbury Cake: 114
spicy yeast buns with currants

Preserved Oranges and Lymonds: 116
orange-lemon marmalade

Candied Roots, Fruits, or Flowers: 118
roots, fruits, and flower petals candied
in rose-water syrup

A Dyschefull of Snowe: 120
rose water and sweetened heavy cream
topped with egg whites and garnished
with sprigs of evergreen

PLANNING THE ELIZABETHAN BANQUET   123

GLOSSARY   125

SUGGESTIONS FOR FURTHER READING   129

INDEX   132

NOTES ON THE ILLUSTRATIONS   136

PREFACE

ONE BLUSTERY DAY last fall, watching the leaves turn color, I found myself thinking about the *Forme of Cury*, that unique cookery manuscript which provided medieval recipes for my first cookbook, *To the King's Taste*. What happened to those exotic soups, pies, and custards after they left the hands of Richard II's cooks?

I remembered reading that a manuscript copy of the *Forme of Cury* had been presented to Queen Elizabeth, and began wondering if the Queen had ever requested that her master cook make use of it. . . . What, in fact, did Elizabeth eat?

That question enticed me to embark upon a second voyage into the history of early English cuisine. But I never quite left the dock: jaunts through library stacks and card catalogues did not produce answers. I found no particular cookery book associated with Elizabeth's household and, to my further dismay, learned that the Queen preferred to dine simply and alone!

However, one thing I noticed during those library trips did intrigue me. The cookbooks of the period all had titles like *A Closet for Ladies and Gentlewomen*, *Delightes for Ladies*, and *The English Hous-wife*. I became curious about the middle- and upper-class cuisine of Tudor England. Did Shakespeare dine as Chaucer had?

I did find answers to that question, and a few fascinating details about Queen Elizabeth to boot.

So here you are: Elizabethan cookery—*puddinges, pyes,* and *piggs petitoes.*

LORNA J. SASS

11

Cest vn miracle rare en l'Europpe chrestienne
De voir Elizabeth la Roine des Anglois,
Mais, cest bien plus de voir, que sa grandeur maintienne
En la paix, les petitz, et les grands, soubz ses lois.

Paul.de la Honce excud.

INTRODUCTION

WHEN ELIZABETH I visited the Earl of Leicester on her progresses throughout the countryside, there were no limits to the earl's desire to please his Queen. In addition to providing an "ambrosiall banket" of more than three hundred different "dishez" daily, he arranged pageants and masques of the most spectacular kind.

On July 18, 1575, after successfully hunting a hart in the surrounding woods, Elizabeth returned to Leicester's Kenilworth Castle. While strolling through the gardens, she came upon a large pool which housed "a swimming mermayd that from top too tayl was an eyghteen foot long." The Queen was promptly informed by Triton, a "servant of Neptune" seated on the mermaid, that the Lady of the Lake was being restrained and mistreated by one very cruel knight: Sir Bruse Sauns Pitee. If the Queen would be kind enough to cast her reflection in the water, she could effect the "deliverauns of the Lady oout of this thralldom."

The moment Elizabeth leaned over the pool's edge, Sir Bruse's power disintegrated. The bands he had wrapped around the Lady of the Lake dissolved, and she floated toward the Queen "upon moovable ilands . . . to declare that her Majestiez prezens hath so graciouslie thus wrought her deliverauns."[1]

Such extravagant display was equaled in kitchen and great hall. When Elizabeth sojourned with Lord North for three days in 1577, his cooks required 140 bushels of wheat, 67 sheep, 34 pigs, 4 stags, 16 bucks, 1,200 chickens, 363 capons, 33 geese, 6 turkeys, 237 dozen pigeons, fish and wild fowl in endless varieties, a carload and two horseloads of oysters, 2,500 eggs, and 430 pounds of butter.[2]

No doubt such bounty prompted Harrison, in his

Description of England in Shakspeare's Youth (1577), to report:

> In number of dishes and change of meat, the nobilitie of England (whose cookes are for the most part musicall-headed Frenchmen and strangers) doo most exceed. . . . They have not onelie beefe, mutton, veale, lambe, kid, porke, conie, capon, pig, or so manie of these as the season yeeldeth: but also some portion of the red or fallow deere, beside great varietie of fish and wild foule, and thereto sundrie other delicates wherein the sweet hand of the Portingale is not wanting.

In fine weather, after the traditional meat and fowl courses of the feast, guests were invited to an outdoor banqueting house of "bowes" (boughs), whose frame sometimes exceeded three hundred feet in circumference. Ivy, holly, and fresh flowers were woven into the branches; grapes, pomegranates, oranges, and melons peeked between streamers of gold cloth.

In this pastoral setting, "banqueting conceits" were set forth to please the eye as well as the palate: mythological scenes of colored marzipan, wild beasts of sugar paste. Trompe l'oeil was the order of the day:

To make a walnut, that when you cracke it, you shall find biskets, and carrawayes in it, or a prettie posey written

Take a piece of your Past royall white, being beaten with Gumtragacant, and mixed with a little fine searsed Cynnamon, which will bring your past into a Walnut shell colour. Then drive it thinne, and cut it into two pieces, and put the one piece into the one half of your mould, and the other into the other. Then put what you please into the nut, and close the mould together, and so make three or foure Walnuts.

To make a dish of snowe

Take a pottle of sweet thicke Creme, and the white of eighte Egges and heate them altogither with a spoone. Then put them into your Creme with a Dishe full of

Rosewater and a dish ful of Sugar with all. Then take a sticke and make it clene, and then cut it in the ende, foure square, and therwith beat all the aforesaide things togither, and ever as it ariseth take it off and put it into a cullander. This doon: take a Platter and set an apple in the midest of it, and stick a thick bush of Rosemarye in the apple. Then cast your Snowe upon the Rosemary and fill your Platter therwith.[3]

(see recipe, p. 120)

Gervase Markham, in *The English Hous-wife* (1615), advised on the special order for presenting these sweets:

You shall first send forth a dish made for shew only, as Beast, Bird, Fish, Fowl, according to invention: then your March-pane, then preserved Fruit, then a Past, then a wet sucket, then a dry sucket, Marmalade, comfets, apples, peares, wardens, Oranges and Lemons sliced, and then wafers, and another dish of preserved fruits, and so consequently all the rest before, no two dishes of one kind, going or standing together, and this will not only appear delicate to the eye, but invite the appetite with the much variety thereof.

A *wet sucket*, or *succade*, was a dish of preserved fruit while dry suckets were candied fruits and vegetables of all kinds (see recipe, p. 119). Particularly popular was the candied sea holly known as erringo root, for it was believed to be an aphrodisiac.

Contemporary accounts of the aging and black-toothed Elizabeth recall that she was constantly chewing *comfets*, sugar-coated whole spices, to freshen her breath. "Let it haile kissing Comfits, and snow Eringoes," said Shakespeare in *The Merry Wives of Windsor*. And so it did.

The "Dyning Parlor"

A German traveler, observing Queen Elizabeth at Greenwich Palace in 1598, reported:

> The Queen dines and sups alone, with very few Attendants, and it is very seldom that any Body, Foreigner or Native, is admitted at that Time, and then only at the Intercession of somebody in Power.[4]

Like his Queen, the Tudor gentleman preferred to leave behind the formality of the great hall and dine in privacy with family and special guests. The architectural response to this growing desire for private dining was the evolution of the "dyning parlor," a small room built adjacent to the hall.[5]

In the dining parlor, where space was limited, radical changes in medieval table style and seating were made of necessity. No longer could the master eat at a separate, raised table, nor was there sufficient room to seat diners along only one side of tables arranged in a U-shape. The single dining table was now placed in the center of the room, with diners on all four sides, as in the modern tradition. Master and mistress presided at the heads of the table, in chairs with high backs; other diners sat on cushioned stools.

The easily dismantled trestle table was still used for servants' meals in the great hall, but a permanent table was more suited to a "dyning parlor." A rectangular joined drawing table was designed with leaves hidden under the top so it could be expanded to nearly double its original size. On a matching square table, food was assembled before it was served. Although the room was sparsely furnished, there might be one or a pair of cupboards on which the family plate was stored and displayed.

The Elizabethans took pride in using their finest serving pieces at mealtime. Tableware was made of a variety of materials: earthenware, wood, pewter, glass, silver, and gold. Trenchers, the bread-plates of the Middle Ages, were now made of either wood or pewter, and often had a small indentation in one corner for salt. Spoons, knives, and goblets were generally of silver, and were available in such quantity that a visiting Italian diplomat commented:

> In one single street named the Strand, leading to St. Paul's, there are fifty-two goldsmith's shops, so rich and so full of silver vessels great and small, that in all the shops in Milan, Rome, Venice, and Florence put together, I do not think there would be found so many of the magnificence that are to be seen in London.[6]

As magnificent as these were, the most highly prized wineglasses were not silver, but Venetian glass. Typically ruby-colored and speckled with gold dust, their bowls were shallow and their stems blown into delicately wrought animal faces. These sculptures of sparkling glass remained on the cupboard until, at mealtime, a diner called for a drink. When the cupful was brought, a guest never drank all of its contents, for that was considered rude; nor was it polite to request the cup more than twice during an ordinary meal.

Napkins were provided for diners, and were either slung over the left shoulder or, if long enough "to make both ends meet," were tied around the enormous Elizabethan ruff. Knives and spoons formed

17

part of each place setting, but forks were still not considered proper eating utensils for a gentleman. In fact, when Thomas Coryat, upon his return from Italy in 1611, expressed enthusiasm for this two-pronged implement, he was considered affected and nicknamed "furcifer." "The Italian," Coryat explained in his *Crudities* (1611), "cannot by any means indure to have his dish touched with fingers, seeing all mens fingers are not alike cleane." "As for us in the country," retorted an English gentleman, "when we have washed our hands after no foul work, nor handling any unwholesome thing, we need no little forks to make hay with our mouths, to throw our meat into them."[7]

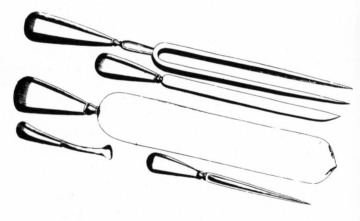

In many households, children were the ones to serve the food, supply guests with extra trenchers, remove and empty "voiders" as they became filled with bones, serve cups of wine and ale, and hold the ewers so guests could wash between courses. For the child sitting at the board's end, a basic rule was to be seen and not heard. F. Seager, author of the *Schoole of Vertue and Booke of Goode Nourture for Chyldren* (1557), was one of many "poets" to teach the rules of table etiquette:

For rudnes it is	thy pottage to sup,
Or speake to any,	his head in the cup.
Thy knife se be sharpe	to cut fayre thy meate;
Thy mouth not to full	when thou dost eate;
Not smackynge thy lyppes,	As comonly do hogges,
Nor gnawynge the bones	As it were dogges;
Suche rudenes abhorre,	Suche beastlynes flie,
At the table behave	thy selfe manerly. . . .
Let not thy tongue	At the table walke,
And of no matter	Neyther reason nor talke.
Temper thy tongue	and belly alwy,
For "measure is treasure,"	the proverbe doth say. . . .
Pyke not thy teethe	at the table syttynge,
Nor use at thy meate	Over muche spytynge;
this rudnes of youth	Is to be abhorde;
thy selfe manerly	Behave at the borde.
If occasion of laughter	at the table thou se,
Beware that thou use	the same moderately.
Of good maners learne	So muche as thou can;
It wyll thee preferre	when thou art a man.[8]

Elizabethan Fare

Aside from the daily round of roasted meats and fowl, most served with interesting sauces (see recipes, pp. 83–88), the Elizabethans enjoyed a wide variety of prepared dishes. For those occasions when she especially wished to impress her guests, the cook was instructed "to make Pies that the Birds may be alive in them, and flie out when it is cut up":

> Make the coffin of a great Pie or pasty, in the bottome whereof make a hole as big as your fist, or bigger if you will. Let the sides of the coffin bee somewhat higher then ordinary Pies, which done, put it full of flower and bake it, and being baked, open the hole in the bottome, and take out the flower. Then having a Pie of the bignesse of the hole in the bottome of the coffin aforesaid, you shal put it into the coffin, withall put into the said coffin round about the aforesaid Pie as many small live birds as the empty coffin will hold, besides the Pie aforesaid. And this is to be done at such time as you send the pie to the table, and set before the guests:

where uncovering or cutting up the lid of the great Pie, all the Birds will flie out, which is to delight and pleasure shew to the company. And because they shall not bee altogether mocked, you shall cut open the small Pie, and in this sort you may make many others, the like you may do with a Tart.[9]

For less flamboyant tastes, there were *simple fricases* of bacon, beef, or pork collops fried with eggs, and *compound fricases* such as tansies, fritters (see recipe, p. 74), pancakes, and *quelquechose* (see recipes, pp. 58, 76). *Carbonadoes*, the latest rage, according to Markham, were "meat broyled upon the coals, and the invention was first brought out of France as appears by the name."

The Italian influence was also evident during the Tudor period, particularly in the widespread use of veal, a meat which never appeared on medieval English menus. In addition to the flesh itself, veal kidney was eaten, either shredded, fried with eggs, and spread on bread for *veal tosts*, or roasted and combined with sweet potherbs and custard in a pie called a *florentine*.

In 1563, by an act of Parliament, Elizabeth proclaimed that her countrymen had to eat fish on Wednesdays, Fridays, and Saturdays. Infraction of her command was punishable by three months' imprisonment or a three-pound fine. This law was grounded in economics, not religion: Elizabeth wished to spark the English shipbuilding industry and force down the price of meat. Judging by the number of recipes for eel and herring pies (see recipes, pp. 42, 44) and fish poached in beer (see recipe, p. 61), she succeeded.

Pies and tarts of all kinds were extremely popular in Elizabethan England. Often the pastry was made with flour, small bits of butter, and hot water or broth (see recipe, p. 108). This dough was kneaded into a stiff paste and then shaped to hold a stuffing without the support of a tin. For sweet fillings, the bottom crust was sometimes flavored with rose water and sugar (see recipe, p. 113).

Considering the quantity and variety of ingredients required in certain recipes, pies and tarts must have been quite large. A *chickin pie*, for example, required whole trussed chickens, and a *minst pye* contained the meat of a leg of mutton in addition to apples, dried fruits, and various other ingredients (see recipes, pp. 52, 48).

Tarts of vegetables like beets (see recipe, p. 68), artichokes (see recipe, p. 66), or beans (see recipe, p. 72) were as common as a *tarte of apples and orenge pilles* (see recipe, p. 98) or a *Warden pie* (see recipe, p. 100). Particularly unusual to our way of thinking was the *spinnage tart* (see recipe, p. 104), made with sugar and served as a sweetmeat for dessert.

Galo di montagna

The Elizabethans often cooked their puddings in containers made of hollowed-out carrots, cucumbers, or turnips (see recipe, p. 70). Such a method proved not only practical, but delicious. Other puddings, such as *rice puddings* and *livering puddinges* (see recipes, pp. 90, 41), were prepared using methods similar to our own.

One of the most fascinating recipes of the period,

21

undoubtedly considered an aphrodisiac, is found in *The Good Huswives Handmaid for Cookerie* (1588):

A tart to provoke courage either in man or woman

> Take a quart of good wine and boile therein two Burre rootes scraped cleane, two good quinces, and a potato roote well pared, and an ounce of Dates, and when all these are boiled verie tender, let them be drawne through a strainer wine and al, and then be put in the yolkes of eight eggs, and the braines of three or fower cocke sparrowes, and straine them into the other, and a little rosewater, and seeth them all with sugar, cinamon and ginger, and cloves and mace, and put in a little sweet butter, and set it upon a chafing dish of coales between two platters, and so let it boile til it be something big.

Who but the already "courageous" would dare to try such a concoction?

The Elizabethan Kitchen Garden

In the opinion of Markham, the good English "hous-wife" had to "have knowledge of all sorts of herbs belonging unto the Kitchin whether they be for the Pot, for Sallets, for Sauces, for servings, or for any other seasoning or adorning." As in the Middle Ages, the category of herbs included vegetables, flowers, and any growing plant whose leaves and stems were used as food.

The Elizabethans loved gardens, and most houses had a flower and topiary garden in the front. Sir

Francis Bacon considered a decorative garden "the Greatest Refreshment to the Spirits of Man." The herb garden, on the other hand, was set on the side and out of sight, "for the many different sents that arise from the herbes, as cabbages, onions, etc. are scarce well pleasing to perfume the lodgings of any house."[10]

Nevertheless, vegetables were coming into their own, and Holinshed, the chronicler of the Tudor period, noted that "melons, pompions, gourdes, cucumbers, radishes, skirets, parsnips, and turnips" were no longer shunned as food of the poor, but were eaten "as deintie dishes at the tables of delicate merchants, gentlemen and the nobilitie who make their provision yearelie for new seeds out of strange countries."

During the sixteenth century, a number of new vegetables were introduced into England and quickly gained popularity: asparagus, artichokes, and spinach, to name a few. Most significant for subsequent years was the importation of sweet and common potatoes. The extremely complex botanical history of these vegetables has never been completely sorted out, but most historians agree that the Spaniards brought the common potato to Europe about 1580 from its native South America. Sir Walter Raleigh, often given credit for that feat, actually conveyed the sweet potato from Virginia to England, and wasn't the first to do so.

The Elizabethan traveler Hakluyt, in his *Voiages and Discoveries* . . . (1589), described the sweet potato as "the most delicate rootes that may be eaten, and doe farre exceed our passeneps or carets." Nevertheless, neither the sweet nor the common potato caught on immediately in England, and few recipes during the first quarter of the seventeenth century make use of them.[11]

Musk melons, eaten raw with pepper and salt or

steeped in wine, were favored. These gourds are described in Gerard's *Herball or General Historie of Plants* (1597) as "of a russet colour and green underneath . . . deep furrowed and ribbed. . . . The inward substance is yellow, which only is eaten." The root vegetable skirret, long and thin, "sweet, white, good to be eaten, and most pleasant in taste," also held a prominent place, as did kidney beans and varieties of peas: rouncial, green and white hasting, Scottish, and Fulham among others. Also known were the Jerusalem artichoke, cardoon, and bucks-horn.

Vegetable dishes were still not commonly mentioned on banquet menus, but the great number of recipes for their preparation indicates that they received considerable attention from cooks. Vegetable dishes fell under the generic title of *sallets*, and they were served raw, boiled, or baked. The importance of giving *sallets* aesthetic appeal is indicated by two recipes from Dawson's *The Good Huswifes Jewell* (1587):

Sallets for fish daies
Onions in flakes laid round about the dishe, with minced carrets laid in the middle of the dish, with boyled Hippes in five partes like an Oken leafe, made and garnished with tawney long cut, with oile and vinegar.
another
Carret rootes being minced, and then made in the dish after the proportion of a Flowerdeluce. Then picke Shrimps and lay upon it with oyle and vinegar.

Markham distinguishes between *simple* and *compound sallets*. To make a *simple sallet*, take:

Chives, Scallions, Radish-rootes, boyled carets, skirrets, and Turnips . . . young Lettice, Cabbage-lettice, Purslane and divers other herbs which may be served simply without any thing but a little Vineger, Sallet Oyle, and Suger: Onions boyled and stript from their rind, and served up with Vineger, Oyle, and Pepper, is a good simple Sallet and so is Samphire, Bean cods,

Sparagus, and Cucumbers served in likewise with Oyle,
Vineger, and Pepper, with a world of others, too tedious
to nominate.

Compound sallets, on the other hand, were made of
"the young Buds and Knots of all manner of whol-
some Herbs at their first springing as red Sage,
Mint, Lettice, Violets, Marigolds, Spinage, and many
other mixed together" (see recipe, p. 79). *Compound
sallets* of boiled greens were often seasoned with
spices and butter, and served on small bread toasts
called *sippets*.

Although flowers were grown primarily for deco-
ration—Queen Elizabeth maintained a waiting-
woman whose sole job it was to strew fresh flowers
in her path—they were used in healing potions and in
cookery as well. Particularly popular was the marigold; its yellow petals were dried and used in broths
and *quelquechose* (see recipe, p. 76). *Compound
sallets* of flowers were preserved by pickling and
used "both for shew and use, for they are more
excellent for taste then for to look on."

Of all ingredients in Elizabethan recipes, rose
water, the distilled water of roses (sometimes damask roses), occurs most frequently. Rose petals and
young buds were often confected in sugar (see recipe,
p. 119) and eaten as a snack or a soothing lozenge.

Sugar and Spice

"All meates and drinkes the which is swete, and that suger is in, be nutrytyve," advised the venerable doctor Boorde in his *Dyetary of Helth* (1542), and the Elizabethans followed this prescription to excess. It is the rare recipe which does not call for sugar in some quantity.

The finest sugar was described by the Tudors as:

> hard, solid, light, exceeding white and sweet, glisning like snow, close and not spungy, melting very speedily in any liquor. Such cometh from Madera in little loaves of three or four pound weight apeece . . . Barbary and Canary sugar is next to that. Your common and coarse sugar is white without and brown within, or a most gluish substance, altogether unfit for candying or preserving, but serving well enough for common syrups and seasoning of meat.[12]

The price of sugar was considerably lower than it had been in the Middle Ages, since the English had begun trading directly with cane growers and were doing much of the refining themselves. Sugar was sold by grocers in loaves: "Scrape it on," the recipes constantly advise us.

The intriguing spices of medieval cuisine—cubeb, galingale, and grains of paradise—were not imported during the Tudor period, and consequently dropped quickly from the recipes. Cinnamon, mace, nutmeg, and anise seed were still used frequently, and Elizabethan cooks showed considerable interest in caraway and cumin. Since the Portuguese had discovered a sea route to the East Indies in 1498, the spice trade was no longer monopolized by the Arabs, and prices were within reach of the middle classes, although still high.

The relative prices of spices and imported dried fruits, rice, and nuts can be seen in the household account book of a Tudor statesman. This entry was made on April 1, 1549:

½ pound mace	6s. 8d.
½ pound cloves	2s. 6d.
1 ounce saffron	20d.
20 pounds currants	8s. 4d.
4 pounds dates	2s.
1 pound ginger	3s. 4d.
½ pound cinnamon	2s. 10d.
6 pounds pepper	14s.
1 pound caraways	14d.
6 pounds almonds	2s.
a quarter of a "hundreth" of great raisins	5s.
3 pounds rice	6d.[13]

Breads and Cakes

The varieties of bread were classified according to the type of flour used, and the fineness of the bolting cloth employed for sifting. Harrison explains:

> The gentilitie commonlie provide themselves sufficientlie of wheat for their owne tables, whilest their household and poore neighbours are inforced to content themselves with rie, or barleie, yea, and in time of dearth, manie with bread made either of beans, peason, or otes, or al altogither. . . .

The best white-wheat bread, called *manchet*, was shaped into small round loaves weighing "eight ounces into the oven and six ounces out." Second-quality bread, or *cheat*, was generally made into larger loaves of whole-wheat flour with the bran removed. *Ravelled* bread contained whole wheat with some quantity of bran, and *browne* bread was prepared with completely unmilled flour. The latter type was sometimes mixed with rye flour to form a *meslin,* or mixed-grain loaf.

Most breads were prepared using ale barm as the *godesgoode,* or leavening agent. The dough was left to rise in a large trough, then kneaded and shaped. The size and quality of each type of loaf was strictly regulated by special bread laws.

Cakes were made with butter, flour, and eggs; the latter were frequently the only leavening agent. Characteristically, cakes were flavored with rose water or a variety of aromatic spices (see recipe, p. 95). They were generally shortbreads, considered perfect when crisp and crumbly.

Beer, Wine, and other Drinks

The Elizabethans loved their drink. A census of alehouses, inns, and taverns taken in 1577 shows that over five thousand drinking establishments existed in Kent, Nottinghamshire, and Yorkshire alone.[14] Even the local parish churches did a lively trade, according to Stubbs' *Anatomy of Abuses in England* (1583):

> In certain townes where dronken Bacchus beares swaie, . . . the church wardens of every parishe, with the consent of the whole parishe, provide halfe a score, or twenty quarters of mault, whereof some they buy of the church stocke, and some is given them of the parishioners themselves . . .; which maulte being made into very strong ale or bere is sette to sale, either in the church or some other place assigned to that purpose. Then, when this is set abroche, well is he that can gete the soonest to it, and spend the most at it. In this kind of practice they continue six weeks, a quarter of a yeare, yea, halfe a yeare together. That money, they say, is to repaire their churches and chappels with, to buy bookes for service, cuppes for the celebration of the sacrament . . . and such other necessaries. . . .

28

Ale, made by brewing malt, had been the popular drink of the medieval period. Although beer was available by the late fifteenth century, Chaucer's contemporaries believed that the hops required for its preparation endangered the health. However, Flemish and Dutch merchants of ingenuity and zeal encouraged the continued importation of hops into England, and by the early sixteenth century they were being grown on an appreciable scale in the south.

Soon beer, the "son of ale," became the most popular English drink. It was prepared in three strengths: single, double, and double-double. Brewers preferred preparing double-double, as they could sell it at a high price. The Queen, however, preferred single, and in 1560, the second year of her reign, ordered that the brewing of double-double be stopped, and that brewers make "as much syngyl as doble beare and more." At one point during Elizabeth's progresses, Leicester wrote to Lord Burleigh: "There is not one drop of good drink here for her. We were fain to send to London and Kenilworth and divers other places where ale was; her beer was so strong and there was no man able to drink it."

Harrison registers similar complaints about drinks available for purchase at the marketplace: "I find . . . such heady ale and beer in most of them, as for the mightinesse thereof among such as seek it out, is commonly called Huffcap, the Mad Dog, Father Whoresonne, and Dragons' Milk. . . ." Alewives were infamous for adding resin and salt to their brews, ruining the flavor so they would keep longer; such adulteration was punishable by fines, but difficult to regulate. As a result, many Elizabethans brewed their own beer at home. From the initial brew, hundreds of varieties were created by the addition of herbs and spices such as sage, betony, mace, and nutmeg.

During Elizabeth's reign, thousands of tons of wine were imported yearly, primarily from France, but from Germany, Italy, Greece, Portugal, and Spain as well. Most highly esteemed were the "mighty great wines" shipped from Bordeaux, and the sweet, rich malmsies of Crete. Little distinction was made among particular vineyards or regions, and wines arriving from the port at Bordeaux were merely labeled red, white, or claret. The latter classification was applied to all wines of a lighter color than red (although they were not necessarily lighter in body), somewhat like our rosé. Claret was the most popular wine for use in cookery.

The wines of Spain were considered the strongest and longest lasting. The name *sack* or *seck* designated an extremely dry Spanish amber wine; *sherry sack* referred to the wines of Jerez. *Sack* was first mentioned in the imported wine lists in 1532, and its popularity throughout England was well established by Elizabeth's reign, as a look at Falstaff's drinking habits quickly reveals.

By 1550, alcohol was being distilled from wine of all qualities. Labeled "burning water," it was considered an essential ingredient in the healthy diet. The drinks prepared with distilled waters were classified in the *Newe Jewell of Health* (tr. 1576) as laudable, comfortable, commendable, and singular. Particularly popular was *spiritus dulcis*, made of *sack*, spirit of roses, and sugar candy. Absinthe was prepared with dried leaves of wormwood in equal parts with malmsey and "burning water thrice distilled." Distilled waters were called *cordials* in the belief that they stimulated the workings of the heart.

The Elizabethans, like their ancestors, drank *hippocras*, hot mulled wine, and the fermented fruit ciders of apples and pears. They also drank mead, which in the late medieval period had gone out of favor.

Shakespeare's words in *Richard II* suddenly come to mind:

> [We cannot] cloy the hungry edge of appetite by imagination of a feast. . . .

On to the recipes.

NOTES TO THE INTRODUCTION

1. John Nichols, *The Progresses and Public Processions of Queen Elizabeth*, vol. I (London, 1823), p. 457.

2. L. F. Salzman, *England in Tudor Times* (New York, 1969), pp. 85–86.

3. "To make a walnut . . ." is from *A Closet for Ladies and Gentlewomen* (London, 1608). "To make a dish of snowe" is in A. W., *A Booke of Cookry* (London, 1584).

4. Paul Hentzner, *A Journey into England in the Year 1598*. Printed in *Fugitive Pieces on Various Subjects*, vol. II (London, 1765), p. 276.

5. This discussion of the dining parlor leans heavily on R. W. Symonds, "The 'Dyning Parlor' and its Furniture," *The Connoisseur*, 113 (1944), pp. 11–17. See also "The Evolution of the Cupboard," *The Connoisseur*, 111–12 (1943), pp. 91–99, by the same author.

6. Charlotte Sneyd, ed., *A Relation, or rather A True Account of the Island of England . . . about the year 1500* (New York, 1968), pp. 42–43.

7. See Thomas Coryat, *Crudities*, vol. I (London, 1901), pp. 236–37, and Nicholas Breton, "The Court and Country, or A Briefe Discourse betweene the Courtier and Country-man of the Manner, Nature, and Condition of their Lives" (London, 1618). Printed in *Inedited Tracts* by The Roxburghe Library (London, 1868), p. 201.

8. See F. J. Furnivall, *Early English Meals and Manners* (London, 1868), p. 232.

9. This recipe is found in *Epulario, or The Italian Banquet* (London, 1598).

10. Letter from Peter Kemp to Sir Thomas Cecil (1561) quoted in Alicia Amherst, *A History of Gardening in England* (London, 1896), p. 135. The Holinshed quote which follows is in Amherst, p. 136.

11. For the definitive work on the subject, see Redcliffe N. Salaman, *The History and Social Influence of the Potato* (Cambridge, 1949).

12. Quoted in Colin Clair, *Kitchen and Table* (New York, 1964), p. 114. Unfortunately, the precise source is not given.

13. F. G. Emmison, *Tudor Food and Pastimes* (London, 1964), p. 46.

14. Unless otherwise noted, the source of information on ale and beer is H. A. Monckton, *The History of English Ale and Beer* (London, 1966), *passim*. The section on Tudor wine relies heavily on André L. Simon, *History of the Wine Trade in England*, vol. II (London, 1906), *passim*.

RECIPES

The following recipes were chosen from cookery books published between 1550 and 1620, the years which roughly span the reign of Queen Elizabeth (1558–1603) and the life of William Shakespeare (1564–1616). The recipes have not been translated into modern English since their language is fairly close to our own, but you will find the meanings for all unusual words and phrases in the Glossary.

The Elizabethans were fond of cooking food in edible containers, and many of the recipes are for pies. Since we are unaccustomed to eating two or three varieties of pie in one meal, you may wish to eliminate the bottom pastry and bake the filling in a casserole dish. If you decide to exclude a top crust, however, be sure to cover the food as it cooks.

But don't let me discourage you: pies and tarts were among the highlights of Elizabethan cuisine, and the cooks went to great lengths to make them visually exciting as well as smacking of good flavor. Bottom crusts were sometimes molded into the shapes of animals, and lids were decorated with pastry cutouts of coats of arms and other "inventions." So, after preparing your crust, let your imagination run wild with any extra dough.

In the cookery of this period, egg yolks and rose water are ubiquitous ingredients. Save the separated whites (you may freeze them until needed) for *snowe* (see recipe, p. 120), or paint the unbaked bottom crust of your pies with them to prevent the pastry from getting soggy when filled. Rose water is available in most gourmet shops.

For their main meal, Elizabethans ate two courses, one of meat and the other of fowl; vegetables were incidental and rarely mentioned on menus. The classifications in this cookbook are therefore somewhat arbitrary and were made solely for the convenience of the modern reader. Many of the categories overlap, so feel free to serve as an entrée a dish labeled appetizer, or vice versa.

The modern adaptations are offered merely as guidelines for your own interpretive efforts. For the most part, I have remained as true as possible to the original recipes. But occasionally, to enrich taste, shorten preparation time, or exercise a rebellious spirit, I have deviated slightly from the instructions.

In the words of the French gastronome Brillat-Savarin: "The discovery of a new dish is more beneficial to humanity than the discovery of a new star." I trust you'll agree after making your own voyage into Elizabethan cuisine.

BON APPÉTIT

APPETIZERS

A gentil man, er he take a cooke, wyll examine hym, howe many sortes of meats, potages, and sauces, he can perfectly make.

SIR THOMAS ELYOT
The Boke Named The Governour (1531)

To boyle a Rack of Veale on the French Fashion   Cut it into steakes. Cut a Carrot or Turnip in pieces, like Diamonds, and put them into a Pipkin with a pinte of white wine, parsley bound in a Fagot, a little Rosemary, and large Mace, and a sticke of Sinamon: pare a Lemmon, or Orenge, and take a little grose Pepper, halfe a pound of Butter: boyle all together until they be enough: when you have done, put in a little Sugar, and Vergis. Garnish your Dish as you list.

JOHN MURREL
A New Booke of Cookerie

HEARTY VEAL SOUP

The sixteenth-century doctor Andrew Boorde commented in his *Dyetary:* "Pottage is not so much used in all Christendom as it is used in England."

Here is a hearty soup which the English borrowed from the French. You may wish to reduce and thicken the liquid and serve this dish with rice or noodles as a stew.

$2\frac{1}{2}$ pounds lean breast of veal, cut into $1\frac{1}{2}$-inch cubes, bones intact
4 tablespoons butter
1 large leek, sliced in thin rings, green tail removed
4 medium carrots, cut into 2-inch lengths
4 medium turnips, peeled and cut into eighths
2 cups dry white wine
2 cups chicken broth or stock
small bunch fresh parsley
2 cinnamon sticks, broken into small pieces
4–6 thin slices orange or lemon peel
20 black peppercorns
cheesecloth and string
$\frac{1}{8}$ teaspoon ground rosemary
$\frac{1}{2}$ teaspoon salt
pinch mace
$\frac{1}{2}$ teaspoon sugar
garnish: chopped parsley

1. Brown veal in 2 tablespoons butter in a large soup pot. Remove veal and set aside.
2. In same pot, brown leek, carrots, and turnips in additional 2 tablespoons butter.
3. Return veal to pot. Pour wine and broth over veal and vegetables.
4. Make a *bouquet garni* by placing parsley, cinnamon, peels, and peppercorns in cheesecloth. Tie *bouquet garni* securely with string. Place in pot.
5. Add rosemary, salt, mace, and sugar.
6. Bring soup to a boil. Reduce flame and stir a few times.
7. Cover and simmer about 1 hour and 15 minutes, or until meat is tender. Check and adjust seasoning after about 45 minutes.
8. Serve in soup bowls, and garnish with parsley.

SERVES 4

Five flocks of sheepe coulde scarce mainteine good mutton for his house.

GEORGE GASCOIGNE
The Poesies (1575)

How to make Fartes of Portingale   Take a peece of a leg of mutton. Mince it smal and season it with cloves, mace, pepper, and salt, and Dates minced with currants: then roll it into round rolles, and so into little balles, and so boyle them in a little beef broth and so serve them foorth.

The Good Huswives Handmaid

SPICY MUTTONBALL SOUP

The Portuguese influence was felt strongly during the Tudor period, since England relied on the merchants of Portugal to provide most of the sugar, spices, and other luxury imports from the East. Much of England's economy was based on the exportation of wool; hence, primarily old sheep were slaughtered for food, and mutton was more commonly eaten than lamb.

Here is a hearty soup whose full-bodied flavor belies the ease of preparation. The *fartes* (pronounced fár-tess) are meant to be light and airy, and should therefore be eaten immediately after they are cooked.

> 6 cups beef broth or stock
> 1 pound ground lean lamb or mutton
> ¼ teaspoon cloves
> ⅛ teaspoon mace
> ½ teaspoon salt
> ⅛ teaspoon freshly ground pepper
> 1½ tablespoons currants
> 1½ tablespoons pitted, finely minced dates
> garnish: minced fresh parsley

1. Bring stock to a boil, then reduce to simmer.
2. In a bowl, combine remaining ingredients, being careful to sprinkle spices and salt evenly over meat.
3. Roll mixture into about a dozen small balls.
4. Place meatballs in simmering stock. Cover pot and continue to simmer for 10 minutes or until meatballs are done.
5. Skim excess fat from top.
6. Serve hot with a garnish of parsley.

SERVES 6

This geare cometh even in puddyng time rightlie.

JOHN HEYWOOD
Proverbes in the Englishe Tongue (1546)

How to make Livering Puddinges Take the Liver of a Hogge, and give it three or fower waumes over the fier. Then either grate it or choppe it verye small, and take a little grated bread and two egges well beaten, whites and all, and Currans, Nutmegges, Pepper, and Salte, and Hogges suet.

The Good Hous-wives Treasurie

CHICKEN LIVER PÂTÉ

"Puddyng time" was any time that puddings were to be had, hence a time when one was in luck. Well, it's pudding time for you: here is an easy, pleasantly spiced pâté made with chicken livers. It would be suitable as an hors d'oeuvre, appetizer, or luncheon entrée.

1 pound chicken livers
1 quart salted, boiling water
1 tablespoon bread crumbs
2 eggs, lightly beaten
$\frac{3}{4}$ teaspoon freshly grated nutmeg
$\frac{1}{8}$ teaspoon freshly ground pepper
salt to taste
1 tablespoon melted beef suet or rendered chicken fat
2 tablespoons currants
garnish: currants, bay leaves, whole-wheat toast

1. Plunge chicken livers into boiling water. Cover and cook over medium heat for 10 minutes.
2. Drain livers. Push them through the fine blade of a food mill, or pound them into a paste with a mortar and pestle.
3. In a bowl, combine remaining ingredients.
4. Add mixture to ground liver, and stir to distribute evenly.
5. Place "pudding" in a small serving bowl and chill at least 2 hours.
6. Before serving, plant a few bay leaves in the "pudding," and scatter currants around them.
7. Serve with small squares of whole-wheat toast.

YIELD: $1\frac{1}{2}$ cups

Whosoever have hym best, is no more sure of hym, than he that hath an ele by the tayle.

DUKE OF NORFOLK
State papers of Henry VIII (1524)

How to bake Eeles After you have drawn your Eeles, chop them into small pieces of three or four inches, and season them with Pepper, Salt, and Ginger, and so put them into a Coffin with a good lump of butter, great Raisons, Onions small chopt, and so close it, bake it, and serve it up.

GERVASE MARKHAM
The English Hous-wife

DEEP-DISH EEL AND ONION PIE

Eel was a popular fish on meatless Lenten days, and recipes abound for its preparation in soups, stews, and pies. Perhaps because of its unusual shape, a fascinating mythology developed about this snake-like fish. The *Hortus Sanitatis*, a compendium of ancient lore translated into English during the Renaissance, states:

> The Eel . . . is hard to skin, and very difficult to kill, as it lives even after it has been skinned; it is disturbed by the sound of thunder. It is most easily caught when the Pleiades have set. And they say that in the Eastern river Ganges, Eels are gendered with feet to walk on the land. Eels live for eight years and they exist without water for six days while the North-east wind blows, but less while the South wind blows. Among all Eels there is no male nor female, and they gender neither live creature nor egg, as they are neuter.

Here is a simple and delicious pastry-covered eel stew for which your fishmonger has to do most of the work. Plan to serve each portion in its own dish, and warn your guests to be on the lookout for stray bones.

**2 pounds eel, cleaned, skinned, backbone
 removed (about 1¼ pounds, ready to bake)**
¼ cup lemon juice
½ teaspoon salt
⅛ teaspoon powdered ginger
⅛ teaspoon freshly ground pepper
2 tablespoons butter
2 medium onions, minced
2 tablespoons raisins
9-inch unbaked pie pastry lid
1 tablespoon milk

1. Chop eel into 1-inch lengths.
2. In a bowl, combine lemon juice, salt, ginger,
   and pepper. Toss eel pieces in this mixture.
3. Melt butter in a skillet, and sauté onions until
   translucent.
4. Add onions and raisins to eel mixture. Stir to
   distribute ingredients evenly.
5. Place mixture in a 9-inch pie plate. Cover with
   pastry lid and crimp edges. Paint milk on lid.
   Slash lid in a few places to allow steam to
   escape.
6. Bake at 375° for 1 hour.
7. Serve hot.

SERVES 6–8

**A foule olde riche widowe, whether wed would ye,
Or a younge fayre mayde, beyng poore as ye be? In
neither barrell better hearyng, quoth hee.**

JOHN HEYWOOD
Proverbes in the Englishe Tongue (1546)

A Herring Pye Take white pickled Herrings of one nights
watering, and boyl them a little. Then take off the skin, and
take onely the backs of them, and pick the fish clean from
the bones. Then take good store of Raisins of the Sun, and
stone them, and put them to the fish. Then take a warden or
two, and pare it, and slice it in small slices from the core,
and put it likewise to the fish. Then with a very sharp
shredding knife shred all as small and fine as may be: then
put to it good store of Currants, Sugar, Cinamon, slic't
Dates, and so put it into the coffin, with good store of very
sweet Butter, and so cover it, and leave onely a round
vent-hole on the Top of the lid, and so bake it like pies of
that nature: When it is sufficiently bak't, draw it out, and
take Claret Wine, and a little Verjuyce, Sugar, Cinamon, and
sweet Butter, and boyl them together: then put it in at the
vent-hole, and shake the pye a little, and put it againe into
the Oven for a little space, and so serve it up, the lid being
candied over with Sugar, and the sides of the dish trimmed
with Sugar.

GERVASE MARKHAM
The English Hous-wife

HERRING-FRUIT PIE

White herring was traditionally gutted and washed
as soon as it was caught, left in brine for a day, then
drained and barreled. Red herring, after it was
cleaned and soaked in brine for a short period, was
strung by the head on little wooden spits and hung
in a special chimney to be smoked for 24 hours.
Herring pies were particularly popular during Lent
and on fish days.

This combination of ingredients may surprise you,
but don't be surprised if you like it.

8-inch unbaked pie pastry shell and lid
1 pound pickled herring, boned and cut into
 chunks
cold water
1½ quarts boiling water
1 large pear, peeled, cored, and sliced
1 tablespoon currants
1 tablespoon raisins
2 tablespoons pitted, minced dates
pinch sugar
pinch salt
¼ teaspoon cinnamon
2 tablespoons dry white wine
1 tablespoon butter, cut into small pieces
1 teaspoon sugar

1. Bake pie shell at 425° for 10 minutes. Let cool.
2. Rinse pickled herring in cold water. (If you are
   using the type of pickled herring which comes
   with onions, you may include the onions in this
   recipe.)
3. Plunge herring into boiling water. Cook for 1
   minute. Remove and drain.
4. In a bowl, combine remaining ingredients
   except butter and teaspoon sugar. Add herring.
5. Using slotted spoon to strain off excess liquid,
   transfer mixture from bowl to pie shell.
6. Dot mixture with butter.
7. Cover with pastry lid and crimp edges. Slash
   lid in a few places to allow steam to escape.
8. Sprinkle lid with sugar.
9. Bake at 375° for 1 hour.

SERVES 6

ENTRÉES

I know no wayes to mince it in love, but directly to say, I love you.

WILLIAM SHAKESPEARE
Henry V (1599)

To make Minst Pyes Take your Veale and perboyle it a little, or mutton. Then set it a cooling: and when it is colde, take three pound of suit to a legge of mutton, or fower pound to a fillet of Veale, and then mince them small by themselves, or together whether you will. Then take to season them halfe an unce of Sinamon, a little Pepper, as much Salt as you think will season them, either to the mutton or to the Veale, take eight yolkes of Egges when they be hard, half a pinte of rosewater full measure, halfe a pound of Suger. Then straine the Yolkes with the Rosewater and the Suger and mingle it with your meats. If ye have any Orrenges or Lemmans you must take two of them, and take the pilles very thin and mince them very smalle, and put them in a pound of currans, six dates, half a pound of prunes. Laye Currans and Dates upon the top of your meate. You must take two or three Pomewaters or Wardens and mince with your meate . . . ; if you will make good crust put in three or foure yolkes of egges, a little Rosewater, and a good deale of Suger.

The Good Hous-wives Treasurie

MINCEMEAT PIE

Mincemeat pies, traditionally part of the Elizabethan Christmas dinner, were so named for the minced meat, suet, and apples within. This version is full of taste surprises: here a bit of fresh orange peel, there a morsel of apple or veal. I'll not mince words: it's delicious, and no one will wish to make mincemeat of the cook!

48

8-inch unbaked pie pastry shell
¾ pound ground veal
¼ pound beef suet, finely chopped
2 cups minced apple
¾ teaspoon salt
⅛ teaspoon freshly ground pepper
⅛ teaspoon freshly grated nutmeg
⅛ teaspoon mace
¼ teaspoon cloves
¼ teaspoon cinnamon
3 egg yolks, hard-boiled
1 tablespoon rose water
1 teaspoon sugar
1 teaspoon finely minced orange peel
1 teaspoon finely minced lemon peel
2 tablespoons currants
8 dates, pitted and minced
8 prunes, pitted and minced

1. Bake pie shell at 425° for 10 minutes. Let cool.
2. In a bowl, combine veal, suet, apple, salt, and spices, being careful to distribute dry ingredients evenly.
3. Mash egg yolks with rose water and sugar.
4. Add egg yolks and remaining ingredients to meat mixture. Mix as you would a meat loaf.
5. Place mixture in pie shell, smoothing top.
6. Cover with aluminum foil and bake at 350° for 50 minutes. Remove foil and bake for an additional 10 minutes.
7. Serve immediately.

SERVES 4–6

For the order of my life, it is as civil as a civil orange.

THOMAS NASHE
Strange Newes (1593)

To boyle a Capon with Orenges after Mistres Duffelds Way
Take a Capon and boyle it with Veale, or with a marie bone, or what your fancy is. Then take a good quantitie of that broth, and put it in an earthen pot by it selfe, and put thereto a good handfull of Currans, and as manie Prunes, and a fewe whole maces, and some Marie, and put to this broth a good quantitie of white Wine or of Clarret, and so let them seeth softlye together: Then take your Orenges, and with a knife scrape of all the filthinesse of the outside of them. Then cut them in the middest, and wring out the juyce of three or foure of them, put the juyce into your broth with the rest of your stuffe. Then slice your Orenges thinne, and have uppon the fire readie a skillet of faire seething water, and put your sliced Orenges into the water and when that water is bitter, have more readie, and so change them still as long as you can find the great bitternesse in the water, which will be five or seven times, or more. If you find need: then take them from the water, and let that runne cleane from them: then put close orenges into your potte with your broth, and so let them stew together till your Capon be readie. Then make your sops with this broth, and cast on a little Sinamon, Ginger, and Sugar, and upon this lay your Capon, and some of your Orenges upon it, and some of your Marie, and towarde the end of the boyling of your broth, put in a little Vergious, if you think best.

The Good Huswives Handmaid

CAPON IN ORANGE SAUCE

The only thing I know about Mistress Duffeld is that she was a genius when it came to cooking capons. Here is Renaissance England's version of orange sauce, served to best advantage over rice, noodles, or buttered toast. The original was made with the Seville orange, therefore the concern for boiling and changing water to eliminate bitterness.

**1 4–5 pound fowl (capon or chicken), cut into
12–15 pieces, bones intact**
salt to taste
$\frac{1}{3}$ cup flour
2–3 tablespoons butter
$\frac{3}{4}$ cup chicken broth or stock
$\frac{1}{2}$ cup dry white wine
$1\frac{1}{2}$ cups orange juice
$2\frac{1}{2}$ teaspoons dried orange peel
generous pinch mace
$\frac{1}{8}$ teaspoon ground rosemary
$\frac{1}{8}$ teaspoon cinnamon
$\frac{1}{8}$ teaspoon ground ginger
1 teaspoon sugar
1 cup pitted prunes
$\frac{1}{2}$ cup currants
garnish: orange slices

1. Sprinkle pieces of fowl lightly with salt; then dredge them in flour.
2. In a heavy skillet, melt 2 tablespoons butter. Brown fowl, adding more butter if needed. Set aside.
3. In a large enameled pot, combine remaining ingredients. Bring to a boil. Reduce flame to simmer.
4. Add browned fowl. Cover and simmer about 1 hour or until fowl is tender. Check seasoning.
5. Skim off fat or, if time permits, place pot in refrigerator for a few hours; then remove solidified fat.
6. Reheat if necessary. Arrange pieces of fowl attractively on a bed of rice, noodles, or buttered toast, and spoon orange sauce on top. Garnish with orange slices.

SERVES 6–8

I woulde not have him to counte his Chickens so soone before they be hatcht.

STEPHEN GOSSON
The Ephemerides of Phialo (1579)

To bake a Chickin Pie   To bake a Chickin Pie after you have trust your Chickins, broken their legges and breast bones, and raised your crust of the best past, you shall lay them in the coffin close together with their bodies full of butter: Then lay upon them and underneath them currants, great raysons, prunes, cinamon, suger, whole mace and salt: then cover all with great store of butter and so bake it. After powre into it the same liquor you did in your marrow bone Pie* with the yelkes of 2 or 3 egges beaten amongst it: And so serve it forth.

GERVASE MARKHAM
The English Hous-wife

*In the preceding recipe, for marrow-bone pie, Markham calls for a "liquor" of white wine, rose water, sugar, cinnamon, and vinegar mixed together.

CHICKEN PIE

In addition to preparing a pie, this recipe suggests the possibility of roasting a chicken and using the dried fruit, spices, butter, and brown sugar as a stuffing. I've tried it both ways, and would be hard put to tell you which I liked better.

9-inch unbaked pie pastry (see instructions
  below)
½ cup dry white wine
½ teaspoon cinnamon
⅛ teaspoon mace
¼ cup currants
¼ cup raisins
½ cup pitted prunes
1 2½-pound chicken, cut into 12–15 pieces,
  bones intact
½ teaspoon salt
1 tablespoon butter, cut into small pieces
1 tablespoon brown sugar

1. Line the bottom of a 2-quart ovenproof
   casserole dish with pie pastry, and bake at 425°
   for 10 minutes. Let cool.
2. In a large bowl, mix wine and spices.
3. Add dried fruits, stir, and let stand about 15
   minutes.
4. Toss chicken pieces in wine and fruits,
   sprinkling with salt as you mix.
5. Place mixture in pie shell. Dot with butter.
6. Cover and bake for 45 minutes at 350.°
7. Uncover and sprinkle with brown sugar. Bake,
   uncovered, for an additional 15 minutes or until
   chicken is done.
8. To serve, scoop out chicken with serving spoon,
   scraping up a section of pie crust with each
   portion.

SERVES 4

Like the table of a countrey Justice . . . sprinkled over with all manner of . . . Sallads, sliced Beef, Giblets, and Petitoes.

FRANCIS BEAUMONT and JOHN FLETCHER
The Woman Hater (1607)

How to boyle Piggs Petitoes Take your Pigs feets, and the Liver, and Lightes, and cut them in small pieces. Then take a little mutton broth and apples sliced, corance, sweet butter, vergious, and grated Bread. Put them altogither in a little pipkin, with Salt, and Pepper. Perboyle your petitoes, or ever you put them in your Pipkin. Then when they be redy: serve them upon sippets.

A. W.
A Book of Cookrye

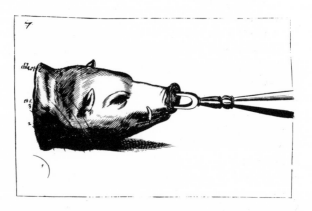

PIGS' FEET AND APPLES

As a nation, we aren't terribly fond of eating pigs' feet. We become squeamish about eating certain parts of animals, primarily, I believe, because they are arbitrarily or irrationally eliminated from our common food vocabularies.

54

For those of you who still hesitate to taste pigs' feet, it might help to think of them as pigs' *petitoes.*

4 pigs' feet, each quartered
water
4 cups lamb or beef stock
¼ cup vinegar
1 cup white wine
½ teaspoon salt
⅛ teaspoon freshly ground pepper
1 tablespoon butter
2 large apples, peeled, cored, and sliced
2 tablespoons currants
4 slices toast
garnish: sprigs of parsley, apple slices

1. In a large saucepan, cover pigs' feet with water and bring to a boil.
2. Reduce heat and simmer for 10 minutes.
3. Drain pigs' feet and run them under cold water.
4. In the same saucepan, combine remaining ingredients except toast. Bring to a boil.
5. Add pigs' feet. Reduce flame, cover pot, and simmer for 2 to 3 hours or until meat is tender. Skim off fat about every 30 minutes.
6. Spoon mixture over toast. Garnish with sprigs of parsley and apple slices.

NOTE: You may wish to separate pigs' feet from other ingredients and serve them hot or cold on a bed of apple slices, decorated with currants.

SERVES 4

[It is] a preatti Poole wherin be good Luces and Tenchis.

JOHN LELAND
The Itinerary (1552)

A Pudding in a Tench Take your Tench and drawe it very clene and cut it not over lowe. Then take beets boyled, or Spinage, and chop it with yolks of hard Eggs, Corance, grated Bread, Salt, Pepper, Sugar and Sinamon, and yolks of rawe Egges, and mingle it togither, and put it in the Tenches belly. Then put it in a platter with faire water and sweet butter and turn it in the Platter and set it in the Oven, and when it is inough: serve it with sippets and poure the licour that it was boiled in upon it.

A. W.
A Book of Cookrye

BAKED STUFFED FISH

Any hollowed-out space, such as the cavity of an eviscerated fish, invited the Elizabethan cook to create a "pudding" for the stuffing. In this case, the tench, a fresh-water fish related to carp, is filled with an unusual stuffing of spinach or beets, egg yolks, spices, and currants for a striking, tasty dish.

> 1 5–6 pound carp or fish of your choice,
>   cleaned and ready for baking
> salt and freshly ground pepper to taste
> 2 cups cooked, chopped spinach or diced
>   beets
> 2 egg yolks
> ¼ teaspoon salt
> ¼ teaspoon cinnamon
> pinch sugar
> ¼ cup bread crumbs
> 2 tablespoons currants
> 1 cup white wine or water
> 3 tablespoons melted butter
> 6 slices toast

56

1. Sprinkle the inside of the fish with salt and pepper.
2. In a bowl, combine remaining ingredients except wine, butter, and toast.
3. Place mixture in fish cavity and close with skewers or toothpicks.
4. Set stuffed fish in a large roasting pan. Pour wine or water over fish.
5. Brush fish liberally with melted butter and pour remaining butter into pan.
6. Bake uncovered at 400° about 1 hour or until fish flakes, basting about every 20 minutes.
7. Carve fish and serve each portion on a slice of toast, spooning wine sauce over top.

SERVES 6

Ile teach . . . to make caudels, Jellies . . . cowslip sallads, and kickchoses.

THOMAS DEKKER
If it be not Good the Divil is in It (1612)

To make any Quelquechose To make a Quelquechose, which is a mixture of many things together, take the Eggs and break them, and do away one half of the Whites, and after they are beaten, put them to a good quantity of sweet Creame, Currants, Cinamon, Cloves, Mace, Salt, and a little Ginger, Spinage, Endive, and Mary-gold flowers grossely chopt, and beat them all very well together. Then take Pigges Pettitoes slic'd and grossely chopt. Mix them with the Eggs, and with your hand stirre them exceeding well together. Then put sweet butter in your Frying-panne, and being melted, put in all the rest, and fry it brown without burning, ever and anon turning it, till it be fryed anough. Then dish it up upon a flat plate, and so serve it forth. Onely here is to be observed, that your Pettitoes must be very well boyled before you put them into the Frycase.

And in this manner, as you make this Quelquechose, so you may make any other, whether it be of flesh, small Birds, sweet Roots, Oysters, Musles, Cockles, Giblets, Lemons, Oranges, or any Fruit, Pulse, or other Sallat herb whatsoever, of which to speak severally, were a Labour infinite, because they vary with mens opinions. Onely the composition and work is no other than this before prescribed, and who can do these, need no further instruction for the rest.

GERVASE MARKHAM
The English Hous-wife

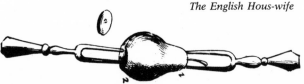

OYSTER-LAMB CASSEROLE

This recipe for *quelquechose* (kickshaws) invites a combination of "whatever," and therefore gave me the liberty to create a new dish and have my own special renaissance in the kitchen. Oysters with mutton is a typically delicious Elizabethan notion; the asparagus or artichokes is my idea. For a *quelquechose* with parsnips, see page 76.

> **1 pound lean shoulder of lamb, cut into small chunks and seasoned with salt and pepper**
> **1 tablespoon butter**
> **1 tablespoon lemon juice**
> **1$\frac{1}{2}$ dozen shucked oysters in their own juice**
> **1 additional tablespoon butter, cut into small pieces**
> **1 pound fresh asparagus *or* 1 package frozen artichoke hearts**
> ***beurre manié:* 1$\frac{1}{2}$ tablespoons flour blended into 1$\frac{1}{2}$ tablespoons soft butter**
> **salt and pepper to taste**

1. In a heavy skillet, brown lamb in 1 tablespoon butter.
2. In a bowl, stir lemon juice into oysters.
3. Combine lamb (with pan drippings) and oysters (with their own juice) in an ovenproof dish.
4. Dot mixture with small pieces of butter.
5. Cover tightly with aluminum foil and bake at 425° for 15 minutes.
6. Meanwhile, cook asparagus or artichoke hearts. Reserve in a warm place.
7. With a slotted spoon, remove oysters and lamb from their liquid. Reserve in a warm place.
8. Pour liquid into saucepan. Heat to boiling. Add *beurre manié*, stirring vigorously over high flame until sauce thickens.
9. Check seasoning. Add salt and pepper to taste.
10. On a serving platter, arrange asparagus or artichoke hearts decoratively over oyster-lamb mixture.
11. Pour sauce over mixture and serve piping hot.

SERVES 3–4

She that in wisedome never was so fraile
To change the Cods-head for the Salmons taile.

WILLIAM SHAKESPEARE
Othello (*1604*)

To seeth Fresh Salmon   Take a little water, and as much
Beere and salt, and put thereto Parsley, Time and Rose-
marie, and let all these boyle togethere. Then put in your
Salmon, and make your broth Sharpe with some Vinigar.

The Good Huswives Handmaid

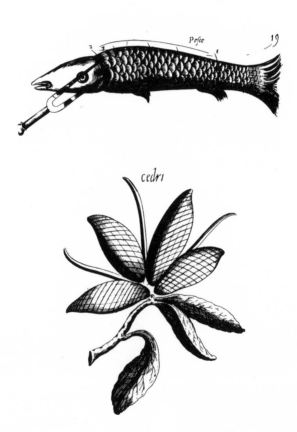

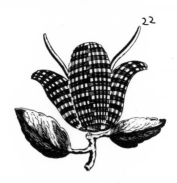

POACHED SALMON

Since the Elizabethans were prohibited from eating meat on Wednesdays, Fridays, Saturdays, and during Lent (a total of over half the days of the year), an easy and delicate preparation like the one opposite must have been eaten quite frequently. The beer and herbs impart subtle accents of flavor to the fish.

> ¾ **cup water**
> ¾ **cup beer**
> **2 tablespoons minced fresh parsley**
> ¼ **teaspoon dried rosemary leaves**
> ⅛ **teaspoon dried thyme**
> ¼ **teaspoon salt**
> **vinegar to taste**
> **4 fish steaks (salmon, halibut, striped bass, etc.)**
> **garnish: sprigs of parsley**

1. In a saucepan large enough to hold fish steaks, combine all ingredients except fish. Bring to a boil; reduce heat and simmer for 5 minutes.
2. Check seasoning.
3. Place fish steaks in saucepan. Cover and poach fish for 10 minutes or until it flakes.
4. Remove fish and serve with garnish of parsley.

SERVES 4

We may picke a thousand sallets ere wee light on such another hearbe.

WILLIAM SHAKESPEARE
All's Well That Ends Well (1601)

To bake an Olive-Pye To make an excellent Olive Pye: take sweet hearbs, as Violet leaves, Strawberry leaves, Spinage, Succory, Endive, Tyme and Sorrel, and chop them as small as may be, and if there be a Scallion or two amongst them, it will give the better taste. Then take the yolks of hard Eggs, with Currants, Cinamon, Cloves, and Mace, and chop them among the hearbs also; Then having cut out long Olives of a leg of Veal, roule up more than three parts of the hearbs so mixed within the Olives, together with a good deal of sweet butter. Then having raised your crust of the finest and best paste, strow in the bottom the remainder of the hearbs, with a few great Raisins, having the stones pickt out. Then put in the Olives, and cover them with great Raisins, and a few Prunes: then over all lay good store of butter, and so bake them. Then being sufficiently bak't, take Claret Wine, Sugar, Cinamon, and two or three spoonfuls of Wine Vinegar, and boyl them together, and then drawing the Pye, at a vent in the top of the lid, put in the same, and then set it into the Oven again a little space, and so serve it forth.

GERVASE MARKHAM
The English Hous-wife

STUFFED VEAL SCALLOPS

An olive pie is not what it sounds like: there are no olives in it—at least not the green and black varieties familiar to us. Renaissance olives are slices of meat, usually beef, mutton, or veal, rolled up around a stuffing of herbs, greens, and hard-boiled egg yolks. The olives are then set on a bed of cooked greens to create a visually appealing and festive dish. The violet and strawberry leaves add an interesting, faintly bitter taste which effectively sets off the mild veal and its stuffing.

9-inch unbaked pie pastry shell
7 cups trimmed and chopped raw greens
   (spinach, chicory, endive, sorrel), washed
2 scallions, minced
1 tablespoon dried strawberry leaves
1 tablespoon dried violet leaves
$\frac{1}{2}$ teaspoon thyme
$\frac{1}{4}$ cup dry white wine or rosé
$\frac{1}{2}$ teaspoon salt
3 egg yolks plus 2 whites, hard-boiled and
   finely chopped
2 additional tablespoons wine
1 tablespoon currants
$\frac{1}{4}$ teaspoon cinnamon
pinch cloves
pinch mace
salt to taste
$\frac{1}{2}$ pound veal cutlets, pounded very thin and
   cut into 6–8 pieces
1 tablespoon butter, cut into small pieces
1 tablespoon raisins
5–6 prunes, pitted and minced
1 additional tablespoon butter, cut into small
   pieces

1. Bake pie shell at 425° for 10 minutes. Reduce temperature to 350° and bake for an additional 5 minutes. Let cool.
2. Place freshly washed (moist) greens, scallions, strawberry and violet leaves, and thyme in a large enameled pot. Sprinkle with ¼ cup wine and salt.
3. Cover and steam over high heat about 3 minutes or until greens wilt. Place wilted greens in a colander to drain.
4. In a bowl, prepare stuffing of chopped eggs, wine, currants, and spices. Add ½ cup wilted greens, chopped very fine, and salt. Mix thoroughly.
5. Place about 2 tablespoons stuffing on each piece of cutlet; set a small piece of butter on stuffing, and wrap meat around it so that ends of meat overlap slightly. Set aside.
6. Add raisins and prunes to remainder of wilted greens. Mix well. Place mixture in pie shell.
7. Arrange stuffed cutlets on greens in an attractive design.
8. Dot with additional tablespoon of butter.
9. Cover tightly with aluminum foil.
10. Bake at 375° for 20 minutes or until veal is cooked.
11. Remove foil and serve as you would a pie.

SERVES 6–8

Meaſure
in wine, com
forteth.

Exceſſe.
walketh wan-
tonly.

SIDE DISHES

The Artichocke groweth like in the heade unto the Pine apple.

THOMAS HILL
The Profittable Arte of Gardening (*1563*)

To make an Artichoak Pye   Take the bottoms of six Artichoaks Boyled very tender, put them in a dish, and some Vinegar over them. Season them with Ginger and Sugar, a little Mace whole, and put them in a Coffin of Paste. When you lay them in, lay some Marrow and Dates sliced, and a few Raisons of the Sun in the bottom, with a good store of Butter. When it is half baked, take a Gill of Sack, being boyled first with Sugar, and a peel of Orange. Put it into the Pye, and set it into the Oven again, till you use it.

attributed to SIR HUGH PLATT
The Accomplisht Ladys Delight

ARTICHOKE PIE

Hakluyt points out in his *Voiages and Discoveries of the English Nation* (1589) that the artichoke was a relatively new foodstuff for the Elizabethans. "In time of memory," he claims, "things have bene brought in that were not here before, as . . . the Artichowe in time of Henry the eight."

Artichokes were most commonly eaten boiled in broth with pepper and salt, but there are a few recipes for artichoke pies like this one. This pie would be suitable as an appetizer or a side dish at dinner, or as a luncheon entrée.

9-inch unbaked pie pastry shell
2 9-ounce packages frozen artichoke hearts or bottoms
$\frac{1}{4}$ cup dry sherry
$1\frac{1}{4}$ teaspoons sugar
$\frac{1}{8}$ teaspoon powdered ginger
$\frac{1}{2}$ teaspoon dried orange peel
pinch mace
vinegar to taste
$\frac{3}{4}$ cup pitted, minced dates
$\frac{1}{4}$ cup raisins
1 tablespoon bone marrow, cut into pieces
1 tablespoon butter, cut into pieces.

1. Bake pie shell at 425° for 10 minutes. Reduce temperature to 375° and bake for an additional 5 minutes. Let cool.
2. Cook artichokes according to directions on package, but reduce boiling time to 2 minutes. Drain artichokes.
3. In a bowl, combine remaining ingredients except butter and marrow.
4. Toss artichokes in this mixture until they are thoroughly coated. Let stand for 30 minutes, stirring occasionally.
5. Place mixture in pie shell, making sure that solid ingredients are evenly distributed.
6. Dot with butter and marrow.
7. Cover tightly with aluminum foil and bake at 375° for about 30 minutes or until artichokes are tender.

SERVES 6–8 AS APPETIZER OR
4–6 AS ENTRÉE

Would you be ever fair and young? Stout of teeth, and strong of tongue? Tart of palat? Quick of ear?

BEN JOHNSON
Volpone (1605)

How to make Lumbardy Tarts   Take beets, chop them small, and to them put grated bread and cheese, and mingle them wel in the chopping. Take a few corrans, and a dishe of sweet butter, and melt it. Then stir al these in the butter, together with three yolkes of egges, sinamon, ginger, and sugar, and make your tart as large as you will, and fill it with the stuffe, bake it, and serve it in.

The Good Huswives Handmaid

BEET TART

Before the sixteenth century, white and green beets were cultivated for their stalks and leaves, which were used as potherbs. In Renaissance England, the red or Roman beet, known today as beetroot, became popular. It is praised with enthusiasm by the herbalist Gerard:

> The red Beet, boyled and eaten with oyle, vinegre and pepper, is a most excellent and delicat sallad. . . . What might be made of the red and beautifull root (which is preferred before the leaves, as well in beautie as in goodnesses) I refer unto the curious and cunning cooke, who no doubt when hee had the view thereof, and is assured that it is both good and wholesome, will make thereof many and divers dishes, both faire and good.

Lombardy tarts were named for the Roman beet stuffing. The cook who invented this subtle combination of flavors was more than cunning: he was a gourmet. For those "tart [keen] of palat," this beet tart is an exciting side dish on a dinner menu. It would also be a welcome entrée at lunch.

68

8-inch unbaked pie pastry shell
4 cups peeled, diced beets (4–5 medium
   beets)
2 tablespoons bread crumbs
2 tablespoons melted butter
2 tablespoons currants
3 egg yolks, beaten
1 tablespoon brown sugar
$\frac{1}{4}$ teaspoon cinnamon
$\frac{1}{4}$ pound mild cheese (i.e., Emmenthaler,
   Monterey Jack), grated
$1\frac{1}{2}$ teaspoons finely minced fresh ginger

1. Bake pie shell at 425° for 10 minutes. Let cool.
2. In a bowl, combine beets with remaining
   ingredients and mix well to distribute evenly.
3. Place filling in pie shell. Cover tightly with
   aluminum foil.
4. Bake at 375° about $1\frac{1}{2}$ hours or until beets are
   tender and can be easily pierced with a fork.
5. Serve warm.

SERVES 6–8 AS SIDE DISH,
4–6 AS ENTRÉE

Euery thing hath an end, and a pudding hath two.
THOMAS NASHE
Four letters confuted (*1592*)

How to make a Pudding in a Turnep Root Take your
Turnep root: and wash it faire in warme water: and scrape
it faire, and make it holow as you doo a Caret root, and
make your stuffe of grated Bread, and Apples chopt fine.
Then take Corance, and hard Egges, and season it with
Sugar, Sinamon, and Ginger, and yolkes of hard Egges, and
so temper your stuf, and put it into the Turnep. Then take
faire water, and set it on the fire, and let it boyle or ever you
put in your Turneps. Then put in a good piece of sweete
Butter, and Claret wine, and a little Vinagre, and Rosemarye, and whole Mace, Sugar, and Corance, and Dates
quartered, and when they are boyled inough: then wil they
be tender. Then serve it in.

A. W.
A Book of Cookrye

TURNIPS STUFFED
WITH APPLES

Most puddings in Elizabethan England had two
"ends," since they were boiled in hogs' guts and
served as sausages. But intestines were difficult to
clean and troublesome to fill, so inventive cooks
sought more practical containers: hollowed-out carrots, cucumbers, and turnips during the Renaissance
and, in later years, the cabbage leaf.

> **2 white turnips, each the size of a large apple**
> **(or 3 medium turnips)**
> **salt to taste**
> **1 cup peeled, minced apple**
> **2 tablespoons currants**
> **2 egg yolks, hard-boiled**
> **2 tablespoons bread crumbs**
> **$\frac{1}{8}$ teaspoon salt**
> **$\frac{1}{4}$ teaspoon cinnamon**
> **$\frac{1}{8}$ teaspoon powdered ginger**

70

1 tablespoon brown sugar
1 cup water
½ cup dry white wine or rosé
1 tablespoon butter
dash vinegar
⅛ teaspoon ground rosemary
pinch mace
8 dates, pitted

1. Peel the turnips, and flatten them by slicing off both top and bottom so that they can stand upright on either end. Cut each turnip in half horizontally.
2. With a sharp knife, cut a deep circle ⅛ inch from the rim of each half as if you were carving a grapefruit. With the knife or the sharp point of a potato peeler, lift out bits of turnip meat until each half looks like a small bowl. (If you wish, dice these excess pieces of turnip and serve them raw in a salad, or carve them into fanciful shapes and use them as garnishes.) Sprinkle each turnip half lightly with salt.
3. In a bowl, combine apple, currants, egg yolks, bread crumbs, salt, cinnamon, ginger, and brown sugar. Heap mixture into each turnip half.
4. In a large enameled pot, bring water and wine to a boil. Add butter, vinegar, and spices. Stir.
5. Reduce heat to simmer. Place stuffed turnips in pot; each should stand on its flattened bottom.
6. Cover and simmer for 50 minutes or until turnips can be easily pierced with a fork. About 5 minutes before turnips are done, add dates to simmering liquid.
7. Serve stuffed turnips in a bowl, placing 1 or 2 boiled dates on each. Spoon wine sauce over them.

SERVES 2–4

Cut the cake: who hath the beane shall be kinge; and where the peaze is she shall be queene.

Anonymous description of a spectacle at Sudely (1592)

Tart of Beanes Take beanes and boyle them tender in fayre water. Then take them oute and breake them in a morter and strayne them with the yolkes of foure egges and curde made of mylke. Then ceason it up with suger and halfe a dysche of butter and a lytle synamon and bake it.

A Proper Newe Booke of Cokerye

KIDNEY BEAN TART

It was the custom, on Twelfth-night, to appoint as king of the company, the man "who hath the beane" in his piece of cake.

The kidney bean is a New World vegetable native to South America. It gained popularity quickly during the Renaissance, and was most often served boiled and buttered as part of a *sallet*. Beans were primarily food for the poor, and in the words of one Elizabethan playwright: "Hunger maketh hard beanes sweet." But this recipe reveals the delicate sweetness of the vegetable even to those who aren't hungry.

> $2\frac{1}{4}$ cups dried kidney beans
> 1 quart salted water
> 2 tablespoons butter
> $\frac{1}{4}$ cup cottage cheese
> 2 egg yolks
> $\frac{1}{8}$ teaspoon salt
> 1 tablespoon brown sugar
> $\frac{1}{4}$ teaspoon cinnamon
> salt to taste
> garnish: thin slices of peeled apple, brown
>   sugar, cinnamon

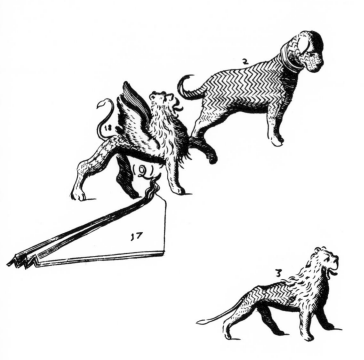

1. Pick over and wash beans.
2. Bring salted water to a boil. Add beans. Cover pot and reduce to medium heat. Cook about 1 hour or until beans are soft.
3. Drain beans. Add butter, and stir to melt and distribute it evenly.
4. In a bowl, combine remaining ingredients and stir to blend. Add this mixture to beans. Mix well.
5. Check seasoning, adding salt to taste.
6. Arrange apple slices attractively on top, sprinkling them lightly with brown sugar and cinnamon.
7. Bake in a covered ovenproof dish at 350° for 40 minutes.

SERVES 6

O Clinias . . . the very fritter of fraud, and seething pot of iniquitie.

SIR PHILIP SIDNEY
Arcadia (*1580*)

To make Fritters of Spinnedge Take a good deale of Spinnedge, and wash it cleane. Then boile it in faire water, and when it is boiled, then take it forth and let the water runne from it. Then chop it with the backe of a knife, and then put in some egges and grated bread, and season it with sugar, sinamon, ginger and pepper, dates minced fine, and currants, and rowle them like a ball, and dippe them in butter [sic] made of Ale and flower.

THOMAS DAWSON
The Good Huswifes Jewell

SPINACH-DATE FRITTERS

The word *fritter* is related to the Latin *frigere*, "to fry," and during the Renaissance was the generic name for any fried food. That spinach came into vogue as a foodstuff in the sixteenth century is attested by Turner in his herbal of 1568: "Spinage or spinech is an herbe lately found and not long in use." Although the true etymology of the word *spinach* is not understood, the Elizabethans believed that it was "so called because his seede is prickly." These tasty fritters make a good snack or hors d'oeuvre.

> **1 pound fresh spinach**
> **2 eggs, lightly beaten**
> **¼ teaspoon salt**
> **⅛ teaspoon freshly ground pepper**
> **¼ teaspoon brown sugar**

$\frac{1}{4}$ teaspoon cinnamon
$\frac{1}{4}$ teaspoon powdered ginger
$\frac{3}{8}$ cup bread crumbs
2 tablespoons currants
$\frac{1}{4}$ cup pitted, finely minced dates
vegetable oil for frying

FOR BATTER:
$\frac{1}{2}$ cup flour
$\frac{1}{2}$ cup plus 2 tablespoons ale

1. Wash and trim spinach and put in a heavy pot without draining.
2. Steam spinach by covering pot and setting over medium heat for 1–2 minutes or until leaves begin to wilt.
3. Drain spinach in colander, and cool to room temperature.
4. Chop spinach finely, place in paper towels, and squeeze out excess moisture.
5. In a bowl, combine eggs, seasonings, and bread crumbs. Mix until well blended.
6. Add currants, dates, and chopped spinach. Stir to distribute evenly.
7. In a bowl, prepare batter by combining flour and ale and stirring until smooth. Mixture should have the consistency of thick pancake batter.
8. In a heavy skillet, heat about $\frac{1}{2}$ inch oil to sizzling.
9. Shape spinach mixture into small patties.
10. Place spinach patties, a few at a time, in batter, and remove each with a slotted spoon (allow excess batter to drip off).
11. Fry fritters in oil for about 3 minutes on each side or until golden.
12. Drain on paper towels. Serve hot.

YIELD: about 20 small fritters

I shall rise again, if there be truth in eggs, and butter'd parsnips.

JOHN FLETCHER
The Woman's Prize (1625)

To make any Quelquechose . . . and in this manner, as you make this Quelquechose, so you may make any other, whether it be of flesh, small Birds, sweet Roots, Oysters, Musles, Cockles, Giblets, Lemons, Oranges, or any Fruit, Pulse, or other Sallat herb whatsoever, of which to speak severally, were a Labour infinite, because they vary with mens opinions. Onely the composition and work is no other than this before described; and who can do these, need no further instruction for the rest.

GERVASE MARKHAM
The English Hous-wife

PARSNIPS AND MARIGOLDS IN ORANGE JUICE

My second *quelquechose* is based on that "sweet Root," the parsnip. I got the idea to boil parsnips in orange juice from the Elizabethans, who like their capon prepared that way (see recipe, p. 50). When using dried marigolds, gently pluck the petals from their green base. Discard the base, as it is bitter-tasting.

76

1½ cups orange juice
1 teaspoon dried orange peel
1 tablespoon butter
1 tablespoon dried marigold petals
⅛ teaspoon cinnamon
1 teaspoon honey
1 pound parsnips, scraped and cut into
⅛-inch discs
beurre manié: 1 tablespoon flour blended into
1 tablespoon butter
garnish: orange slices

1. In a large saucepan, combine all ingredients except parsnips and *beurre manié*. Stir and bring to a boil.
2. Add parsnips. Cover and reduce heat to medium.
3. Cook for 35 minutes or until parsnips are tender but firm.
4. Remove parsnips with a slotted spoon.
5. Bring liquid in pot to a fast boil. Add *beurre manié*, stirring rapidly with a wire whisk until sauce thickens. Check seasoning.
6. Replace parsnips in pot and toss to coat.
7. Place in serving bowl and garnish with orange slices.

SERVES 3–4

There was no Sallet in the lines to make the matter savoury.

WILLIAM SHAKESPEARE
Hamlet (1602)

Compound Sallet To compound an excellent Sallet, and which indeed is usuall at great Feasts, and upon Princes Tables, take a good quantity of blancht Almonds, and with your shredding knife cut them grossely. Then take as many Raisins of the Sun clean washt, and the stones pickt out, as many Figs shred like the Almonds, as many Capers, twice so many Olives, and as many Currants as of all the rest, clean washt, a good handfull of the small tender leaves of red Sage and Spinage: mix all these well together with good store of Sugar, and lay them in the bottome of a great dish. Then put unto them Vineger and Oyl, and scrape more Suger over all: then take Oranges and Lemmons, and paring away the outward pilles cut them into thinne slices. Then with those slices cover the Sallet all over; which done, take the fine thinne leaves of the red Coleflowre, and with them cover the Oranges and Lemmons all over. Then over those Red leaves lay another course of old Olives, and the slices of well pickled Cucumbers, together with the very inward heart of Cabbage lettice cut into slices. Then adorn the sides of the dish, and the top of the Sallet with more slices of Lemons and Oranges, and so serve it up.

GERVASE MARKHAM
The English Hous-wife

RENAISSANCE SALAD

Since Elizabethan food is rather sweet, a piquant salad is essential in your meal, "to make the matter savoury." Using spinach and shredded red cabbage as your base, add small bits of the following ingredients to taste:

> **almond slivers**
> **raisins**
> **minced figs**
> **capers**
> **olives**
> **currants**
> **minced pickles**
> **orange segments**

Prepare a dressing of oil, vinegar, lemon juice, a pinch of sugar, and salt to taste. You will be amazed that such an unlikely combination of ingredients comes to such a felicitous end.

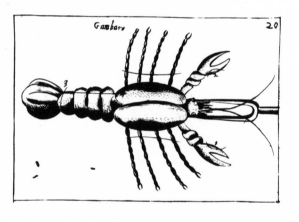

SAUCES

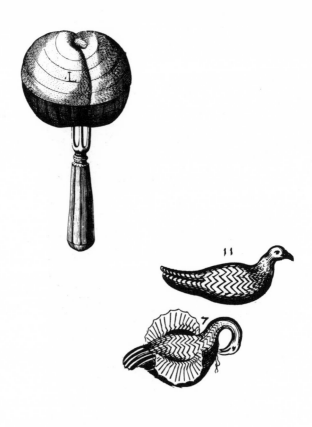

Houngre and thirste is for all thynges the beste sauce in the worlde.

NICHOLAS UDALL
Apophthegmes . . . First gathered by Erasmus (tr. 1542)

Sauce for a Gooce Take Vineger and appells shred very small, two spoonfulls of musterd, a litle Pepper and Salte: and take Suger sufficient to sweeten it. Then boyle it well together.

The Good Hous-wives Treasurie

GOOSE SAUCE

Here is a vinegar-based sauce much in the medieval tradition. Because our vinegars are distilled, they are much more piquant than the turned wine that Elizabethan cooks frequently used. I have therefore used stock for the liquid base, and vinegar as a flavoring. This sauce has a sweet-and-sour quality; it would complement fowl or roasted meat, particularly pork.

> ¾ cup chicken stock
> 2 tablespoons (or more) cider vinegar
> 1 teaspoon mustard, preferably Dijon-style
> 1½ cups apples, pared, cored, and minced
> salt
> pepper
> sugar

1. In a saucepan, combine stock, vinegar, and mustard. Stir to blend.
2. Bring to a boil and add apples.
3. Reduce heat and simmer uncovered for 20 minutes.
4. Check seasoning. Add salt, pepper, and sugar to taste.

YIELD: 1½ cups

83

The Damasin Plummes are woont to be dried and preserved as figges, and are called in English, Prunes.

THOMAS COGAN
The Haven of Health (*1584*)

To make Sauce of dry Proins   Take proines and steep them in clarret wine. Then take out the stones, and stampe them with a few blanched almonds, and a toste of bread soked in the wine wherein the proines were steeped. Stampe all this together, tempering them with a little verjuice and other bastard wine, or sugar which is better. Then straine them, and put spice unto them, specially sinamon.

Epulario, or *The Italian Banquet*

PRUNE SAUCE

This sweet, fruity sauce is particularly delicious with roast chicken or leg of lamb.

> **1 cup dry wine, red or white**
> **1 cup pitted prunes**
> **¼ cup blanched almonds, coarsely ground**
> **1 tablespoon bread crumbs**
> **dash cider vinegar**
> **¼ teaspoon sugar**
> **⅛ teaspoon cinnamon**

1. Combine ingredients in an enameled pan.
2. Bring to a boil. Reduce heat and simmer for 15 minutes.
3. Check seasoning.

YIELD: 1½ cups

Garlyke . . . doth extenuate and cutte grosse humours . . . and heateth all the body.

SIR THOMAS ELYOT
The Castel of Helth (1541)

To make good Garlike Sauce Take blanched almonds well stamped, and being halfe beaten, put as much garlike to them as you think good, and stampe them together, tempering them with water least it bee oiley. Then take crummes of white bread what quantity you will, and soke it either in leane broth of flesh or fish as time serveth: this sauce you may keepe and use with all meats, fat or leane as you thinke good.

Epulario, or *The Italian Banquet*

GARLIC SAUCE

For garlic lovers, this sauce is a must. It is particularly good with baked or broiled seafood, and is just the right consistency for an artichoke stuffing or dip.

- **1 cup blanched almonds**
- **5 large cloves garlic**
- **1 tablespoon ice water**
- **1½ cups chicken stock**
- **2 tablespoons bread crumbs**

1. Place almonds, garlic, and ice water in a blender, and whirl until almonds are coarsely ground.
2. In a saucepan, bring stock to a boil. Add almond mixture and bread crumbs. Stir to blend.
3. Simmer uncovered for 10 minutes, stirring occasionally.

YIELD: 1½ cups

85

As moch for that purpose as to lay unyon to my lytel fynger for the tothe ache.

HENRY BRINKLOW
Complaynt of Roderyck Mors (*c. 1545*)

Sauce for a Roast Capon To make an excellent Sauce for a rost Capon, you shall take Onions, and having sliced and peeled them, boyle them in fair water with Pepper, Salt, and a few bread crummes: then put unto it a spoonfull or two of claret Wine, the juyce of an Orenge, and three or four slices of Lemmon peel: all these shred together, and so pour it upon the Capon being broke up.

GERVASE MARKHAM
The English Hous-wife

ONION SAUCE

Cooking onions in orange juice brings out their sweetness. This sauce is delicious with liver as well as with fowl of any kind. It also makes an unusual topping for hamburgers.

"Beinge eaten in great abundance with meat, onions cause one to slepe soundly," says Sir Thomas Elyot in *The Castel of Helth* (1541).

> **2 cups minced onions**
> **$\frac{1}{4}$ teaspoon finely minced lemon peel**
> **2 tablespoons dry white wine**
> **$1\frac{1}{2}$ cups orange juice**
> **2 tablespoons bread crumbs**
> **salt and pepper to taste**

1. In a heavy saucepan, combine all ingredients except bread crumbs, salt, and pepper.
2. Bring to a boil; then reduce heat to simmer for 10 minutes, stirring occasionally.
3. Add bread crumbs and salt and pepper to taste. Simmer for 2 more minutes.

YIELD: $1\frac{1}{2}$ cups

While sugar hires the taste the brain to drown, and bribes of sauce corrupt false appetite.

PHINEAS FLETCHER
The Purple Island (1633)

Additions unto Sawces Take Orenges and slice them thin, and put unto them White Wine and Rose water, the powder of Mace, Ginger, and Suger, and set the same upon a Chaffing dish of coales, and when it is half boyled, put to it a good lump of butter, and then lay good store of sippets of fine white bread therein, and so serve your Chickens upon them, and trim the sides of the dish with Suger.

GERVASE MARKHAM
The English Hous-wife

ORANGE WINE SAUCE

Served hot, this sauce is a magnificent complement to ham and fowl. Chilled and topped with sweetened whipped cream, it makes a striking dessert.

> **3 oranges**
> **¾ cup dry white wine**
> **¼ cup rose water**
> **generous pinch mace**
> **½ teaspoon finely minced fresh ginger**
> **sugar to taste**

1. Peel oranges and cut them into ⅛-inch slices, discarding seeds. Set aside.
2. In a heavy saucepan, combine wine, rose water, mace, and ginger. Bring to a boil.
3. Reduce heat. Add orange slices and simmer covered for 25 minutes.
4. Check seasoning and add sugar to taste.

YIELD: 2 cups

DESSERTS

He sate upon the Pudding-Boule, the candle for to hold.

Tom Thumb (*1584*)

Rice Puddings Take halfe a pound of Rice, and steep it in new Milk a whole night, and in the morning drain it, and let the Milk drop away, and take a quart of the best, sweetest, and thickest Cream, and put the Rice into it, and boyl it a little. Then set it to cool an hour or two, and after put in the yolkes of half a dozen Eggs, a little Pepper, Cloves, Mace, Currants, Dates, Sugar, and Salt, and having mixt them well together, put in great store of Beef suet well beaten, and small shred, and so put it into the farms, and boyl them as before shewed, and serve them after a day old.

GERVASE MARKHAM
The English Hous-wife

RICE PUDDING

In Elizabethan England, rice was imported, and therefore listed in household account books with other luxury purchases such as spices and almonds. Some rice was ground into fine-quality flour, but much of it was cooked in puddings and pottages. The "farms" mentioned by Markham were shaped containers in which puddings could be boiled and stored. The word *farm* is a sixteenth-century dialect variant of our word *form*.

This rich, creamy rice pudding is a treat either warm or chilled.

90

½ cup white rice
3 cups milk
1 cup heavy cream
2 egg yolks
½ cup brown sugar
generous ⅛ teaspoon salt
⅛ teaspoon white pepper
⅛ teaspoon cloves
⅛ teaspoon mace
¼ cup currants
¼ cup pitted, minced dates
2 tablespoons butter or grated beef suet

1. Combine rice and milk in a heavy enameled pot. Bring to a gentle boil. Cover pot. Reduce heat and simmer about 30 minutes or until rice is soft. Drain off excess milk if you wish.
2. Add cream and bring to a boil. Reduce heat and simmer for 2–3 minutes. Remove from heat.
3. In a bowl, combine remaining ingredients and blend thoroughly.
4. Add mixture to rice and stir to distribute evenly.
5. Cover and cook for 5 minutes over low heat.
6. Serve warm or chilled.

SERVES 6

Our cake's dough on both sides. Farewell.

WILLIAM SHAKESPEARE
The Taming of the Shrew (*1594*)

To make fine Cakes Take a quantity of fine wheate Flower,
and put it in an earthen pot. Stop it close and set it in an
Oven, and bake it as long as you would a Pasty of Venison,
and when it is baked it will be full of clods. Then searce
your flower through a fine sercer. Then take clouted Creame
or sweet butter, but Creame is best: then take sugar, cloves,
Mace, saffron and yolks of eggs, so much as wil seeme to
season your flower. Then put these things into the Creame,
temper all together. Then put thereto your flower. So make
your cakes. The paste will be very short; therefore make
them very little. Lay paper under them.

JOHN PARTRIDGE
The Widowes Treasure

92

FINE CAKES

In the sixteenth century, if your cake was "dough on both sides," your project had certainly failed, for the most delectable cake was a crisp and crumbly, spicy shortbread like this one.

> **6 ounces butter (1½ sticks) at room temperature**
> **½ cup sugar**
> **1 egg yolk, beaten**
> **1¾ cups sifted flour**
> **½ teaspoon cloves**
> **⅛ teaspoon mace**
> **pinch ground saffron**
> **egg white**

1. In a bowl, cream butter. Add sugar and beat until fluffy.
2. Add egg yolk and beat until thoroughly blended.
3. In another bowl, combine sifted flour and spices, stirring to distribute evenly.
4. Sift dry ingredients into bowl containing butter-and-sugar mixture. Combine by stirring or with hands.
5. Press mixture into a 9-inch square baking pan.
6. Brush top lightly with egg white.
7. Bake at 325° for 45 minutes or until cake feels firm when pressed lightly in the center.
8. Cut into squares while cake is still hot.
9. Cool in pan on wire rack.

YIELD: 25 small "cakes"

93

The manner was in old time to weare rings but upon one finger onely, but now adayes . . . every joint by themselves must have some lesser rings and gemmals to fit them.

PHILEMON HOLLAND
Pliny's Historie of the World (tr. 1601)

To make finer Jumbals To make Jumbals more fine and curious than the former, and neerer to the taste of the Macaroon, take a pound of Sugar, beat it fine. Then take as much fine wheat flowre, and mixe them together. Then take two whites and one yolk of an Egge, half a quarter of a pound of blanched Almonds: then beat them very fine altogether, with half a dish of sweet butter and a spoonfull of Rose water, and so work it with a little Cream till it come to a very stiff paste. Then roul them forth as you please: and hereto you shall also, if you please, adde a few dryed Anniseeds finely rubbed, and strewed into the paste, and also Coriander seeds.

GERVASE MARKHAM
The English Hous-wife

JUMBALS

It is thought that the word *jumbal* is derived from *gemel*, a finger ring popular at the time, which could be divided into two separate loops. Jumbals were traditionally shaped as interlacing loops or in fancy knot patterns, but were not always made of rolled dough as the recipe opposite instructs. If you wish, squeeze this batter through a pastry tube to create your own fanciful shapes. But the round cookie with its golden brown edge tastes just as good.

$\frac{1}{2}$ **cup sugar**
2 egg whites
1 egg yolk
$\frac{1}{2}$ **cup sifted flour**
4 tablespoons butter, melted and cooled to warm
1$\frac{1}{2}$ teaspoons rose water
$\frac{3}{4}$ **cup blanched almonds, coarsely ground**
1–2 teaspoons anise or coriander seeds

1. Whip sugar and egg whites with electric or hand beater about 2 minutes or until mixture is the consistency of heavy cream.
2. Add egg yolk, flour, butter, and rose water. Blend thoroughly.
3. Stir in almonds.
4. Drop batter from a teaspoon onto a well greased, lightly floured cookie sheet. Leave at least 1$\frac{1}{2}$ inches between jumbals.
5. Sprinkle tops of jumbals with anise or coriander seeds.
6. Bake at 400° about 12 minutes or until jumbals are golden brown around edges.
7. Remove jumbals from baking sheet immediately and place them on rack to cool.

YIELD: about 20 jumbals

Yes, by Saint Anne, and Ginger shall bee hotte y' thy mouth too.

WILLIAM SHAKESPEARE
Twelfth Night (1601)

Course Ginger Bread   Take a quart of Honey clarified, and seeth it till it be brown, and if it be thick, put to it a dish of water: then take fine crums of white bread grated, and put to it, and stirre it well, and when it is almost cold, put to it the powder of Ginger, Cloves, Cinamon, and a little Licoras and Anniseeds: then knead it, and put it into a mould and print it. Some use to put to it also a little Pepper, but that is according unto taste and pleasure.

GERVASE MARKHAM
The English Hous-wife

GINGERBREAD

Gingerbread was traditionally boiled rather than baked. This recipe is not significantly different from medieval recipes found in fourteenth- and fifteenth-century manuscripts, except for the licorice—a brilliant touch.

Loaves of gingerbread, like squares of quince and other fruit pastes, were often stamped with decorative designs. You may wish to experiment with a cookie or butter press on the top of this little loaf while it is still warm and malleable.

>   1 cup honey
>   generous ¼ teaspoon powdered ginger
>   ⅛ teaspoon ground cloves
>   ⅛ teaspoon cinnamon
>   ⅛ teaspoon ground licorice
>   1¾ cups dry bread crumbs
>   1 tablespoon anise seeds

1. In the top of a double boiler, heat honey. Add spices except anise seeds, and stir to blend.
2. Add bread crumbs and mix thoroughly. Cover and cook over medium heat for 15 minutes. Mixture should be thick and moist.
3. Place gingerbread on a large sheet of waxed paper. Fold up sides of paper and mold dough into small rectangular shape.
4. Sprinkle anise seeds on top and press them gently into dough with the side of a knife.
5. Cover and refrigerate for 2 hours.
6. Serve gingerbread at room temperature in thin slices.

SERVES 8

Provide no great cheare, a couple of Capons, some Fesants, Plovers, an Oringeado-pie, or so.

THOMAS DEKKER
The Honest Whore (1604)

To make a Tarte of Apples and Orenge Pilles Take your orenges, and lay them in water a day and a night, then seeth them in faire water and hony, and let them seeth til they be soft: then let them soak in the sirrop a day and a night: then take them forth and cut them small, and then make your tart and season of apples with sugar, synamon and ginger, and put in a piece of butter, and lay in a course of apples, a course of orenges and so course by course, and season your orenges as you seasoned your apples, with somewhat more sugar. Then lay on the lid and put it in the oven, and when it is almost baked, take rosewater and sugar and boyle them together till it be somewhat thick. Then take out the tart, and take a feather and spread the rosewater and sugar on the lid, and set it into the oven again, and let the sugar harden on the lid, and let it not burn.

The Good Huswives Handmaid

ORANGE AND APPLE PIE

Oringeado, or candied orange peel, was a favorite Elizabethan confection, and often made its way into pastries. The Seville orange, rather bitter in flavor, had been imported from Spain and Portugal in small quantities during the Middle Ages, but became more readily available in the sixteenth century. By that time, Portuguese merchants were also trading a sweet variety of orange from Ceylon. The latter grew

98

quickly in popularity and was soon considered the preferred type to preserve.

In this recipe, a delicate hint of bitterness furnished by the honeyed orange peel combines memorably with the mellow flavor of apples.

9-inch unbaked pie pastry shell and lid
5 medium juice oranges
3 cups water
1 cup honey
juice of $\frac{1}{2}$ small lemon
4 medium apples, peeled, cored, and sliced
$\frac{1}{2}$ cup brown sugar
$\frac{1}{8}$ teaspoon salt
generous $\frac{1}{4}$ teaspoon cinnamon
$\frac{1}{8}$ teaspoon powdered ginger
2 tablespoons confectioners' sugar dissolved in 1 tablespoon rose water

1. Bake pie shell at 425° for 10 minutes. Let cool.
2. Slice oranges as thinly as possible, discarding seeds.
3. Combine water, honey, and lemon juice in a large saucepan. Bring to a boil. Add orange slices. Cover, reduce heat, and simmer about 2 hours or until peel is limp and easily chewed.
4. Drain orange slices and set aside.
5. In a bowl, combine brown sugar, salt, and spices. Add apple slices and toss until evenly coated.
6. Place a layer of apple slices in pie shell, then a layer of orange slices. Repeat with remaining fruit.
7. Place pastry lid over filling. Crimp edges and slash lid in a few places to allow steam to escape.
8. Paint lid with rose-water icing.
9. Bake at 350° for 1 hour.

SERVES 8

I would have had him rosted like a warden in brown paper, and no more talk on't.

FRANCIS BEAUMONT and JOHN FLETCHER
The Coxcomb (1612)

A Warden Pie Take the fairest and best Wardens, and pare them, and take out the hard cores on the Top, and cut the sharp ends at the bottom flat. Then boyle them in white Wine and sugar, untill the sirrup grow thick: then take the Wardens from the sirrup in a cleare dish, and let them cool. Then set them into the coffin, and prick cloves in the Tops, with whole stickes of Cinamon, and great store of Sugar as for Pippins: then cover it, and onely reserve a vent-hole. So set it in the Oven and bake it. When it is bak'd, draw it forth, and take the first sirrup in which the Wardens were boyld, and taste it, and if it be not sweet enough, then put in more Sugar, and some Rose-water, and boyl it againe a little: then pour it in at the Vent-hole, and shake the pye well: then take sweet Butter, and Rose-water melted, and with it annoint the pye-lid all over, and then strow on it store of Sugar, and so set it into the Oven again a little space, and then serve it up: and in this manner you may also bake Quinces.

GERVASE MARKHAM
The English Hous-wife

PEAR PIE

The Warden was king among baking pears in Renaissance England, and came in two varieties: white and red. Since Warden pears are no longer cultivated, I have tried this recipe with Anjous and with great success. The pastry lid is draped over the fruit halves to create six sculptured golden mounds in the shape of a rosette. You might wish to try this recipe with quince, as Markham suggests.

10-inch unbaked pie pastry shell and lid
¾ cup white wine
2 tablespoons sugar
⅛ teaspoon cloves
¼ teaspoon cinnamon
**3 large Anjou pears, peeled, halved, and
cored**
1 tablespoon rose water
1 teaspoon melted butter
1 additional teaspoon rose water
1–2 tablespoons brown sugar

1. Bake pie shell at 425° for 10 minutes. Reduce temperature to 375° and bake for an additional 5 minutes. Let cool.
2. In a heavy enameled saucepan, combine wine, sugar, cloves, and cinnamon. Bring to a boil.
3. Add pear halves. Cover and cook over medium heat for 15 minutes or until fruit is firm but easily pierced with a fork.
4. Drain fruit, reserving wine syrup. Set fruit aside.
5. Add 1 tablespoon of rose water to wine syrup, and stir. Boil briskly for 5 minutes or until syrup is reduced to about ¼ cup. Cool.
6. Toss pear halves in syrup to coat.
7. Set pear halves flat side down in pie shell with narrow ends toward the center. Brush any excess syrup on top.
8. Drape pastry lid over fruit and crimp edges.
9. Combine melted butter and additional rose water. Brush lid with this mixture and sprinkle top with brown sugar. Slash lid in a few places to allow steam to escape.
10. Bake at 375° for 30 minutes or until lid is golden.
11. Serve warm.

SERVES 6

**The naturall place of the Almond is in the hot re-
gions, yet we have them in our London gardens and
orchards in great plenty.**

JOHN GERARD
Herball or General Historie of Plants (1597)

To make a Tart of Almonds   Blanch almonds and beat
them, and strain them fine with good thicke Creame. Then
put in Sugar and Rosewater, and boyle it thicke. Then make
your paste with butter, fair water, and the yolks of two or
three Egs, and so soone as ye have driven your paste, cast
on a little sugar, and rosewater, and harden your paste
afore in the oven. Then take it out, and fill it, and set it in
againe, and let it bake till it be wel, and so serve it.

The Good Huswives Handmaid

ALMOND TART

Almond milk, that popular medieval ingredient, is back again, but this time with the addition of a favorite Elizabethan component: rose water. The filling is crunchy and rich, and tastes best chilled with a topping of strawberry or cherry preserve. For a pie crust based on the recipe opposite, see page 113.

   8-inch unbaked pie pastry shell
   1½ cups blanched almonds, coarsely ground
   1½ cups heavy cream
   1 tablespoon plus 1 teaspoon sugar
   4 teaspoons rose water
   topping: strawberry or cherry preserve

1. Bake pie shell at 425° for 10 minutes. Reduce temperature to 350° and bake for an additional 5 minutes. Let cool.
2. Combine remaining ingredients in a heavy saucepan. Boil gently about 10 minutes, stirring occasionally, until mixture thickens to the consistency of pudding.
3. Pour filling into pie shell.
4. Bake at 350° about 30 minutes or until top is golden.
5. Cool to room temperature on a wire rack. Refrigerate for at least 2 hours.
6. Just before serving, spread a thin layer of preserve on top.

SERVES 6–8

Spinage (so called bicause his seede is prickly) is of two sorts, the male and the female.

RICHARD SURFLET
Maison rustique, or the countrie farme
(*tr. 1600*)

A Spinnage Tart Take good store of Spinage, and boyl it in a Pipkin, with White-Wine, till it be very soft as pap: then take it and strain it well into a pewter dish, not leaving any part unstrained: then put to it Rose-water, great store of Sugar and cinamon, and boyl it till it be as thick as Marmalad. Then let it coole, and after fill your Coffin and adorn it . . .

GERVASE MARKHAM
The English Hous-wife

SWEET SPINACH TART

Spinach "was held in special regard because it had reached the western world much later than the other greenstuff of medieval cookery," comments C. Anne Wilson in *Food and Drink in Britain*. "It came from Persia, through the Arabs, and was first recorded in the west by St. Thomas Aquinas. It arrived too late to acquire any traditional medicinal merits."

Here the Elizabethans treat spinach as a fruit, and with great success. It is fascinating to note how serendipity thrives among cooks who have no preconceived notions about the "proper" use of a particular food.

> **8-inch unbaked pie pastry shell**
> **2½ pounds fresh spinach**
> **¼ cup white wine**
> **½ cup rose water**
> **⅓ cup (or more) sugar**
> **¼ teaspoon cinnamon**
> **generous pinch salt**
> **topping: sliced strawberries and**
>   **confectioners' sugar**

1. Bake pie shell at 425° for 10 minutes. Reduce temperature to 350° and bake for an additional 35 minutes or until done. Let cool.
2. Wash and trim spinach. Put spinach directly into large enameled or aluminum pot without draining. Add wine.
3. Cover and steam spinach over medium flame for 1–2 minutes or until spinach is wilted.
4. Drain spinach and mince very fine.
5. In the same pot, combine rose water, sugar, cinnamon, and salt. Bring to a boil, stirring to dissolve sugar.
6. Add chopped spinach and stir to coat.
7. Simmer over very low flame, stirring occasionally, until all liquid evaporates. Remove from heat and set aside to cool.
8. Fill pie shell with spinach mixture. Arrange sliced strawberries decoratively on top.
9. Chill at least 2 hours.
10. Just before serving, sprinkle lightly with confectioners' sugar.

SERVES 8

MISCELLANEOUS

Of the paste a coffen I will reare.

WILLIAM SHAKESPEARE
Titus Andronicus (*1588*)

Of the Mixture of Paste ... Your course Wheat-crust should be kneaded with hot water, or Mutton broth, and good store of butter, and the paste made stiffe and tough, because that Coffin must be deep.

GERVASE MARKHAM
The English Hous-wife

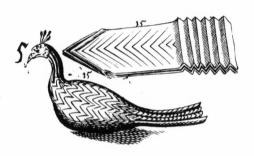

SAVORY PIE PASTRY

This hot-water savory short crust is ideal for moist and liquid fillings. In the Elizabethan period, considerably more flour would have been added and the paste kneaded extremely stiff, so that a pie-crust shape could be formed without the support of a pan. Such a crust is dry and mealy, but you may wish to experiment with it for the visual effect. The following recipe for pie pastry is a tasty compromise.

$\frac{1}{2}$ **pound butter at room temperature**
6 tablespoons boiling water or broth (slightly more if needed)
$2\frac{1}{2}$ **cups sifted flour**
$\frac{1}{2}$ **teaspoon salt**

1. In a large bowl, cut butter into small bits.
2. Pour boiling water or broth over butter and beat immediately with an electric mixer. Beat about 3 minutes or until mixture is creamy and no liquid remains at bottom of bowl. Refrigerate for 30 minutes.
3. In another bowl, combine sifted flour and salt. Sift into bowl with butter.
4. Stir, scraping butter off sides of bowl, until large masses of dough begin to form.
5. Shape 2 balls of equal size by pressing dough together with your hands.
6. Wrap each dough ball in waxed paper and refrigerate at least 1 hour.
7. Roll each piece of dough between 2 pieces of waxed paper.
8. Peel off top paper. Set pie tin upside down on pastry. Slip your hand under waxed paper and flip over both pastry and tin. Press pastry into tin. Peel off waxed paper. (If waxed paper doesn't peel off easily, place covered rolled dough in refrigerator for 15 minutes.)
9. Prick bottom and flute edges.
10. Prebake as directed in your chosen pie recipe.

NOTE: This dough, cooked or uncooked, may be refrigerated for 2–3 days or frozen for 2 months.

YIELD: two 9-inch pie shells

ALE PIE PASTRY

Here is an unusual crust with the added attraction of being easy to roll. It's more the consistency of a crisp bread crust than the flaky pie pastry we're accustomed to today, and would be perfect for a meat or fish pie.

> $\frac{1}{4}$ **cup ale turned flat**
> **6 ounces (1$\frac{1}{2}$ sticks) butter**
> **1 teaspoon sugar**
> **pinch salt**
> **pinch saffron**
> **1 egg, lightly beaten**
> **2$\frac{1}{4}$ cups (or slightly more) sifted flour**
> **rice or dried beans**

1. In a saucepan, heat ale with butter, sugar, salt, and saffron until butter melts. Stir to blend.
2. Pour liquid into a large bowl and cool to room temperature.
3. Add egg and stir.
4. Stir in enough sifted flour to make a moist, but not sticky, dough. A finger pressed deeply into the dough should come out clean. Shape 2 balls of equal size.
5. Wrap each dough ball in waxed paper and refrigerate at least 1 hour.
6. Remove dough from refrigerator, and let stand for 20–30 minutes; then roll each mass of dough between 2 pieces of waxed paper.

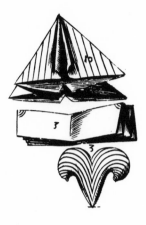

7. Peel off top paper. Set pie tin upside down on pastry. Slip your hand under waxed paper and flip over both pastry and tin. Press pastry into tin. Peel off waxed paper. (If waxed paper doesn't peel off easily, place covered rolled dough in refrigerator for 15 minutes.)
8. Prick bottom and flute edges.
9. Mold aluminum foil to shape of pie shell, pressing it firmly to the sides, and gently covering the fluted rim.
10. Before baking, fill shell with rice or dried beans.
11. Bake at 425° for 10 minutes. Reduce temperature to 350° and bake for an additional 5 minutes. Remove beans and foil. Let cool.

NOTE: This crust requires 15 minutes' prebaking under all circumstances. Because it has a tendency to shrink, it does not work successfully as a top crust. The dough, cooked or uncooked, may be refrigerated for 2–3 days or frozen for 2 months.

YIELD: two 9-inch pie shells

Another Way Then make your paste with butter, fair water, and the yolks of two or three Egs, and so soone as ye have driven your paste, cast on a little sugar, and rosewater, and harden your paste afore in the oven. Then take it out, and fill it, and set it in againe. . . .

The Good Huswives Handmaid

ROSE-WATER PIE PASTRY

This sweet, crunchy crust is ideal for dessert pies.

$\frac{1}{4}$ **pound butter**
1$\frac{1}{2}$ cups sifted flour
1 egg yolk, beaten
ice water
1 teaspoon rose water
1 teaspoon confectioners' sugar

1. In a bowl, work butter into flour with pastry blender until tiny globules of equal size are formed.
2. Place egg yolk in measuring cup. Add enough ice water to equal a little over $\frac{1}{3}$ cup.
3. Sprinkle liquid on flour-butter mixture. Work about ten times with pastry blender, or until large masses of dough begin to form.
4. Place dough on a piece of waxed paper. Touching the paper only, press dough into a large ball. Refrigerate for 1 hour in waxed paper.
5. Roll dough between 2 pieces of waxed paper.
6. Peel off top paper. Set pie tin upside down on pastry. Slip your hand under waxed paper and flip over both pastry and tin. Press pastry into tin. Peel off waxed paper. (If waxed paper doesn't peel off easily, place covered rolled dough in refrigerator for 15 minutes.)
7. Prick bottom and flute edges.
8. Brush pastry with rose water; sprinkle with confectioners' sugar.
9. Prebake as directed in your chosen pie recipe.

NOTE: This dough, cooked or uncooked, may be refrigerated for 2–3 days or frozen for 2 months.

YIELD: one 9-inch pie shell

What man, I trow ye rave. Wolde ye bothe eate your cake, and have your cake?

JOHN HEYWOOD
A Dialogue Conteynyng Proverbes and Epigrammes (1562)

To make a very good Banbury Cake   Take four pounds of currants, and wash and picke them very cleane, and drie them in a cloth: then take three egges and put away one yolke and beate them, and straine them with good barme, putting thereto cloves, mace, cinamon and nutmegges: then take a pinte of creame, and as much mornings milke and set it on the fire till the cold bee taken away: then take flower and put in good store of cold butter and suger. Then put in your egges, barme and meale and worke them all together an houre or more: then save a part of the past, and the rest breake in peeces and worke in your currants: which done, mould your cake of what quantity you please: and then with that past which hath not any currants cover it very thinne both underneath and aloft. And so bake it according to the bignesse.

GERVASE MARKHAM
The English Hous-wife

BANBURY CAKES

Banbury, a town in Oxfordshire, is still famous for its cakes, but today the most popular ones are flavored with rum. Still, Markham's cakes hold their own some three hundred fifty years after they were created. Having no ale barm, we'll use yeast.

Banbury cakes, served warm with butter and jam, are delicious at breakfast or tea.

$\frac{3}{4}$ **cup light cream**
$\frac{1}{2}$ **cup butter**
$\frac{1}{4}$ **cup sugar**
1 teaspoon salt
1 package yeast
$\frac{1}{4}$ **cup tepid water**

2 eggs plus 1 white, lightly beaten
¼ teaspoon freshly grated nutmeg
¼ teaspoon cinnamon
¼ teaspoon cloves
⅛ teaspoon mace
4–4½ cups sifted unbleached white flour
⅓ cup currants
optional icing: 3 tablespoons confectioners'
  sugar dissolved in 1 tablespoon milk and a
  dash anise extract

1. In a saucepan, scald cream. Add butter, sugar, and salt. Stir to dissolve. Pour mixture into a large bowl and cool to lukewarm.
2. In a small bowl, dissolve yeast in water.
3. Add yeast, eggs, and spices to cream mixture.
4. In a large bowl, combine 4 cups of flour and currants, stirring until currants are lightly coated.
5. Add flour and currants to cream mixture. Knead until dough is smooth and elastic, adding more flour if necessary.
6. Place dough in a greased bowl. Cover with a clean, moistened towel, and set bowl in a warm place for dough to rise until doubled in bulk. This will take about 1½ hours.
7. Punch down dough; then knead it again for an additional few minutes.
8. Shape dough into 14–16 2½-inch balls and place them on a greased cookie sheet.
9. Cover "cakes" with a towel, and let rise in a warm place for 1 hour.
10. Bake on cookie sheet at 375° about 25 minutes or until tops are golden.
11. Remove cakes from cookie sheet and cool on a wire rack.
12. Frost with icing, if you wish.

YIELD: 14–16 Banbury cakes

I cannot blame my ladies Unwillingness to part with such marmulade lips.

PHILIP MASSINGER
The Picture (1629)

To preserve Oranges and Lymonds   Take your Oranges and Lymonds large and well coloured, and take a raspe of steele, and raspe the outward rind from them. Then lay them in water three dayes and three nightes. Then boyle them tender and shift them in the boyling to take away their bitterness, and when they bee boyled tenderly, take two-pound sugar clarified with a pint of water, and when your syrope is made, and betwixt hot and cold, put in your Lymonds and Oranges, and there let them bee infused all night. The next morning let them boyle two or three walmes in your Syrope, let them not boyle too long in the sugar, because the rinds will be tough. Take your Lymonds out and boyle your Syrope thicker, and so when it is colde, put them up and keepe them all the yeare.

A Closet for Ladies and Gentlewomen

ORANGE MARMALADE

The word *marmalade* comes from the Portuguese *marmelo*, meaning quince and originally referring to a preserve of this fruit. It soon came to mean a confection made with any cooked fruit. In this recipe, the oranges probably would have been Seville or bitter oranges. If you use sweet oranges, you might wish to add less sugar.

3 large Seville or bitter oranges
2 large lemons
9 cups cold water
8 cups sugar

1. Remove rind from oranges and lemons, and chop it. Shred pulp of fruit, discarding seeds.
2. Place both rind and pulp in a saucepan and add cold water. Let stand at room temperature for 24 hours.
3. Bring to a boil and add sugar, stirring to dissolve.
4. Remove pan from heat and let stand for 24 hours.
5. Bring to a boil again; reduce heat and simmer gently about 2 hours. Then bring to a rapid boil and cook about 20 minutes or until drops run together as they fall off a metal spoon.
6. Skim off surface foam.
7. Pour marmalade into sterile jars and seal with a layer of melted paraffin. (If you plan to refrigerate the marmalade, you need not seal the jars with paraffin.)

YIELD: about 7 cups

The cold Brooke Candied with ice.

WILLIAM SHAKESPEARE
Timon of Athens (1607)

To candy any Roots, Fruits, or Flowers Dissolve sugar, or sugar-candy in Rose-water. Boile it to an height. Put in your roots, fruits or flowers, the sirrop being cold. Then rest a little; after take them out, and boyl the sirrop again. Then put in more roots, etc. Then boyl the sirrop the third time to an hardnesse, putting in more Sugar, but not Rose-water. Put in the roots, etc. the sirrop being cold, and let them stand till they candy.

GERVASE MARKHAM
The English Hous-wife

CANDIED ROOTS, FRUITS, OR FLOWERS

These *suckets* are delicate and easy to make. You'll be amazed how carrots and parsnips turn into candy. If using fresh flowers, choose only unblemished, unsprayed blossoms. Wash them gently in cool water, and drain on paper towels. Do not experiment with wild flowers unless you are certain they are edible.

$1\frac{1}{2}$ cups rose water
$1\frac{1}{2}$ cups sugar
one of the following:
   2 large carrots or parsnips, scraped and sliced into $\frac{1}{8}$-inch discs
   2 small apples or pears, peeled, cored, and cut into $\frac{1}{8}$-inch slices
   1 cup fresh flower petals (trim off white tips which attach petals to stem)

1. In a heavy saucepan, combine rose water and sugar. Bring to a boil.
2. Add vegetable or fruit slices or flower petals. Stir.
3. Return to a boil; reduce heat to a gentle boil and cook for 15 minutes.
4. As soon as sugar begins to caramelize (it will turn light brown), remove pan from heat.
5. Remove vegetable or fruit slices or flower petals, and set them on waxed paper. Refrigerate for 10 minutes.
6. Peel candies off waxed paper and store them in an airtight container.

YIELD: about 2 dozen candies

At Christmas I no more desire a Rose
Then wish a Snow in Mayes new-fangled showes,
But like of each thing that in season grows.

WILLIAM SHAKESPEARE
Love's Labour's Lost (*1588*)

To make a Dyschefull of Snowe   Take a pottell of swete
thycke creame and the whytes of eyghte egges, and beate
them altogether wyth a spone. Then putte them in youre
creame and a saucerfull of Rosewater, and a dyshe full of
Suger wyth all. Then take a stycke and make it cleane, and
than cutte it in the ende foure square, and therwith beate all
the aforesayde thynges together, and ever as it ryseth take it
of and put it into a Collaunder. This done, take one apple
and set it in the myddes of it, and a thicke bushe of Rosemary, and set it in the myddes of the platter. Then cast your
Snowe uppon the Rosemarye and fyll your platter therwith.
And yf you have wafers caste some in wyth all and thus
serve them forthe.

A Proper Newe Booke of Cokerye

SNOW ON AN APPLE TREE

This recipe for a "banqueting conceit" is ideal for a
dramatic holiday drink or dessert. Despite Shakespeare's injunction, you will find it refreshing all
year round.

AS A DRINK:
The following ingredients will serve six, but you
may double or triple the quantities to serve more.

> **3 cups cold heavy cream**
> **3 tablespoons (or more) rose water**
> **3 tablespoons confectioners' sugar**
> **3 egg whites, beaten stiff**
> **garnish: 1 large apple, sprigs of evergreen**

120

1. In a bowl, beat the heavy cream for 1 minute or until it froths.
2. Add rose water and confectioners' sugar. Beat another 30 seconds.
3. Lightly fold in egg whites, reserving a few tablespoons for garnish.
4. Place apple in the center of a punch bowl. (For a colder drink, you may set the punch bowl into a larger bowl of crushed ice.)
5. Pierce apple with sprigs of evergreen.
6. Pour "snow" over apple. Dot evergreen sprigs with bits of reserved egg white.
7. Serve immediately.

AS A DESSERT:

    4 medium apples, cored (peel intact)
    cinnamon
    1 tablespoon butter, cut into pieces
    ¼ cup raisins
    water
    1 cup heavy cream
    1 tablespoon rose water
    1 tablespoon confectioners' sugar
    garnish: sprigs of evergreen

1. Sprinkle the cavity of each apple with cinnamon; then stuff with a bit of butter and 1 tablespoon raisins.

2. Place stuffed apples in an ovenproof baking dish which contains ¾ inch water. Cover tightly.
3. Bake at 375° about 40 minutes or until apples are soft but firm. Remove apples and set aside.
4. In a bowl, combine heavy cream, rose water, and confectioners' sugar. Whip until mixture is stiff.
5. Pierce each baked apple (warm or cold) with a small sprig of evergreen.
6. Place a dollop of flavored whipped cream on top of each.
7. Serve immediately.

SERVES 4

PLANNING THE ELIZABETHAN BANQUET

Since many of the Elizabethan dishes are sweet to the modern palate, the most important thing to remember when planning a menu is to set off the meal with a salad and a dry wine. Otherwise, just choose those dishes which most appeal to you and present them in an order that suits the occasion. Here are some possible combinations:

Suggested Menus

BANQUET FOR FOUR

Baked Eeles

Compound Sallet

Chickin Pie   Piggs Petitoes

Fritters of Spinnedge

Finer Jumbals

Candied Roots, Fruits, or Flowers

BANQUET FOR TEN

Livering Puddinges   Fartes of Portingale

Compound Sallet

Capon with Orenges   Olive Pye

Pudding in a Turnep Root   Artichoak Pye

Warden Pie

Candied Roots, Fruits, or Flowers

BANQUET FOR TWENTY

Herring Pye

Rack of Veale on the French Fashion

Compound Sallet

Pudding in a Tench   Minst Pye

Quelquechose: Oyster-lamb Casserole

Lumbardy Tarts   Tart of Beanes

Spinnage Tart   Course Ginger Bread

Candied Roots, Fruits, or Flowers

GLOSSARY

barme the froth that forms on top of fermenting malt liquors which is used to leaven bread; sometimes referred to as *godesgoode.*

bastard wine a sweet Spanish wine resembling muscatel in flavor.

berberries oblong, red, sharply acid berries known today as barberries.

betony a plant of the mint family believed to have healing qualities.

bucks-horn various plants named for the shape of their leaves or appearance of their branches; also known as Swine's cress; eaten as a salad green.

burre roots the hairy roots of the *burre* reed; dried and pulverized, they were combined with other herbs as a cure for leprosy.

cabbage lettice a variety of lettuce with leaves forming a cabbagelike head.

cardoon a plant in the thistle family closely allied to the artichoke. The fleshy stalks of the inner leaves and the heart are made edible by blanching.

clouted cream clotted cream; cream made by scalding milk until it becomes thick.

coffin pie dough shaped to hold a stuffing.

comfits sweetmeats made of fruit, roots, or seeds by preserving them in sugar. Boorde advises: "Apples shuld be eaten with suger or comfettes . . . bycause of theyr ventosyte."

conneis conies; rabbits.

corance currants. Boorde claims: "smale raysyns of Corans be good for the paynes of the backe and they dothe provoke uryne."

course layer.

cubeb a berry from Java which resembles a peppercorn, but is more aromatic.

currans currants; see *corance.*

damaske water rose water distilled from Damask roses. "Roses be a cordyall," says Boorde, "and doth comforte the herte and the brayne."

drawn cleaned and gutted.

driven your paste rolled your pastry dough thin.

erringo roots   the roots of the sea holly; usually preserved by candying.

fagot   bundle of twigs or herbs tied together.

fallow deer   a species of deer smaller than the stag or red deer, so called for its reddish yellow color.

farms   forms.

fartes   usually refers to balls of light pastry known also as puffs; in this case refers to a meatball.

galingale   an aromatic member of the ginger family; used in medieval sauces.

gill   a measure for liquids; one fourth of a standard pint.

grose pepper   whole or coarsely ground pepper.

grossely   coarsely.

grains of paradise   pungent aromatic seeds of a tropical West African plant; used in making *hippocras* (mulled wine).

gumtragacant   gum arabic; still used today in the manufacture of candy.

haberden   a large, salted cod.

hippes   rose hips.

hundreth   a measure; contemporary equivalent is 108 pounds.

Jerusalem artichoke   the tuber of a sunflower, eaten raw or cooked.

knots   flower beds laid out in intricate designs; hence, the flowers from these gardens used in salads.

lights   the lungs of an animal.

licour   liquid.

luce   a fish of the pike family.

march-pane   marzipan.

marie   rosemary.

marie bone   marrow bone.

mingle   mix.

mudefishe   any type of fish that lives in mud.

muske melon   Gerard explains: "Muske-Melons is like to the common Cucumber in stalks, lying flat upon the ground. . . . The Fruit is bigger. . . . The barke or rinde is of an overworne russet greene colour, ribbed and furrowed deeply, having often chaps or chinks. . . . The pulp or inner substance which is to be eaten is of a feint yellow colour; the middle part whereof is full of a slimie moisture: amongst which is contained the seed."

olives thick slices of meat rolled around a stuffing of cooked egg yolks and a variety of herbs.

oringeado a preserve of oranges; candied orange peel.

pap soft food for infants or invalids; usually made of bread softened with water or milk.

paste pastry dough.

pestell pestle; an instrument for pounding substances in a mortar.

pilles peels; the skin of a fruit.

pipkin a small pot or pan.

pomewater a large juicy kind of apple.

pompion pumpkin.

posset a hot drink of milk, spices, and liquor, often *sack*.

pottel a half gallon.

puff a light pastry or confection.

pulse the edible seeds of leguminous plants cultivated for food, such as peas, beans, and lentils.

raspe a grater; hence, to scrape away.

red sage Gerard explains: "We have in our gardens a kinde of Sage, the leaves whereof are reddish; part of those red leaves are stripped with white, somewhat mixed with greene . . . even as Nature list. . . . The leaves of red Sage put into a wooden dish, wherein is put very quicke coles, with some ashes in the bottome of the dish to keepe the same from burning, and a little vinegre sprinkled upon the leaves lying upon the coles, and so wrapped in linnen cloath, and holden very hot unto the side of those that are troubled with a grievous stitch, taketh away the paine presently."

sammonde salmon.

samphire a plant which grows on sea rocks whose leaves are used in pickling. Gerard claims: "Rocke Sampier hath many fat and thicke leaves somwhat like those of the lesser Purslane, of a spicie taste, with a certain saltnesse."

searsed sifted.

seeth cook; boil.

serce sift.

sippets small pieces of toasted or fried bread, usually served with soup or broth, or used for dipping into gravy; small sops.

skirrets a species of water parsnip no longer cultivated.

sops pieces of bread, sometimes toasted; usually soaked in wine, broth, or gravy.

strow strew; scatter.

stuffe stuffing.

succades *suckets;* sweetmeats of candied fruit or vegetable. Boorde claims: "The rootes of percelly soden tender, and made in a succade, is good for the stone, and doth make a man to pysse." *Succades* were often eaten as a snack.

succory chicory.

sucket see *succades.*

suet the solid fat around the loins and kidneys of certain animals.

tansey a pudding, cake, or egg-based dish flavored with the juice of the herb tansy; it was traditionally eaten at Easter.

tawney a plant named for its tawny-colored (brownish orange) flowers. The greens were eaten in salads.

teg a sheep in its second year, or from the time it is weaned until its first shearing.

tele teal; a small fresh-water fowl.

temper mix; blend.

tench a fresh-water fish of the carp family.

vergis see *verjuyce.*

verjuyce *verjuice;* the acid juice of crab apples.

voider a receptacle for bones and other table waste.

Warden a cooking pear considered ideal for baking.

waumes *walms;* waves of boiling liquid.

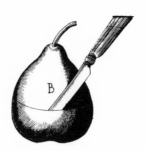

SUGGESTIONS FOR FURTHER READING

Cookery Books:

All of the following were originally printed in London unless otherwise noted. Early editions are available to serious researchers at the British Museum. Most major American libraries own these works on microfilm.

Buttes, H. *Dyets Dry Dinner.* 1599.

A Closet for Ladies and Gentlewomen. 1608.

Dawson, Thomas. *The Good Huswifes Jewell... newly set forth with additions.* 1587.

Epulario, or *The Italian Banquet.* 1598. "Englished" by A. J. from a book by Giovanne de Rosselli published in Italy, 1516.

The Good Huswives Handmaid for Cookerie. 1588.

The Good Hous-wives Treasurie. 1588.

Markham, Gervase. *The English Hous-wife.* 1615.

Murrel, John. *A Newe Book of Cookerie.* 1615.

———. *A Daily Exercise for Ladies and Gentlewomen.* 1617.

Partridge, John. *The Treasurie of Commodious Conceites.* 1584.

———. The Widowes Treasure. 1585.

Platt, Sir High. *Delightes for Ladies.* 1605.

———. (attrib.) *The Accomplisht Ladys Delight.*

A Proper Newe Booke of Cokerye. (Cambridge MS c. 1560). Ed. C. F. Frere. Cambridge, 1913.

The Second Part of the Good Hus-wives Jewell. 1597.

W., A. *A Booke of Cookry Very Necessary for All Such as Delight Therein, Gathered by A. W.* 1584.

General Works:

Amherst, Alicia. *A History of Gardening in England.* London, 1896. Chapters on "Kitchen Gardening Under Elizabeth" and "Elizabethan Garden Literature" demonstrate the aesthetic, medicinal, and culinary import of the garden in Tudor times.

Boorde, Andrew. *Dyetary.* Ed. F. J. Furnivall. Early English Text Society, e.s. 10. London, 1870. The sixteenth-century doctor prescribes some foods for good health and warns vehemently against others.

Clair, Colin. *Kitchen and Table.* New York, 1964. This "Bedside History of Eating in the Western World" contains an entertaining and informative chapter on "Tudors at Table."

Clarkson, Rosetta. *The Golden Age of Herbs and Herbalists.* Dover paperback, New York, 1972. A popular history of herb gardens and the medicinal uses of herbs.

Elyot, Sir Thomas. *The Castel of Helth.* London, 1541. Scholars' Facsimiles and Reprints, New York. A sixteenth-century treatise on "the conservation of the body of mankynde, within the lymitation of helth," much in the style of Boorde.

Emmison, F. G. *Tudor Food and Pastimes.* London, 1964. Drawing on original documents of Sir William Petre, a Tudor secretary of state, this book concentrates on food, drink, and leisure-time entertainments.

_____. *Tudor Secretary.* Cambridge, 1961. The biography of Sir William Petre with chapters on "Food and Drink" and "Household."

Gerard, John. *Leaves from Gerard's Herball.* Ed. Marcus Woodward. Dover paperback, New York, 1969. An abridged edition of Gerard's fascinating *Herball or General Historie of Plantes,* which first appeared in 1597.

Harrison, William. *Description of England in Shakspere's Youth.* London, 1577. Ed. F. J. Furnivall. The New Shakspere Society. London, 1877. A gossipy and charming account of life and times in the Tudor period, including a section on "Food and Diet of the English."

Nichols, John. *The Progresses and Public Processions of Queen Elizabeth.* 3 vols. London, 1823. We follow the Queen around the countryside as she is entertained extravagantly by loyal subjects. Descriptions are taken primarily from contemporary accounts.

Pearson, Lu Emily. *Elizabethans at Home.* Stanford, 1957. A well documented study of the domestic life, rearing of children, and social customs.

Rohde, Eleanour. *The Old English Herbals.* Dover paperback, New York, 1971. The history of herbals in England, with special chapters on Tudor herbalists Turner, Gerard, and Parkinson.

130

Salzman, L. F. *England in Tudor Times*. New York, 1969. A general and well illustrated introduction to home and town life during the period.

Seager, H. W. *Natural History in Shakespeare's Time*. London, 1896. An entertaining dictionary of foods and animals replete with contemporary lore and literary allusions.

Simon, André L. *The Star Chamber Dinner Accounts*. London, 1959. A chatty dictionary of Tudor foods, and lists of provisions purchased daily to prepare meals for Elizabeth's statesmen.

Symonds, R. W. "The 'Dyning Parlor' and its Furniture." *The Connoisseur*, 113 (1944), 11–17. A fascinating, well illustrated essay on the transition from great hall to dining room, and on the furniture designed to meet new needs.

Tusser, Thomas. *Five Hundred Pointes of Good Husbandrie*. London, 1557. Ed. Payne and Herrtage. London, 1878. A charming treatise, in rhyming couplets, on the most effective methods for planting and harvesting crops, and caring for animals.

Wilson, C. Anne. *Food and Drink in Britain*. London, 1973. An invaluable scholarly reference to the eating habits of the British through the ages, replete with footnotes and an extensive bibliography.

Younger, William. *Gods, Men and Wine*. London, 1966. A well researched guide to the drinking habits of man from ancient times to the present, with a special chapter on the Renaissance.

INDEX

Ale, 29
Ale pie pastry, 110
Almond cookies, 95
Almond tart, 103
Apple tree, snow on an, 120
Apples
  candied, 119
  and orange pie, 98
  pigs' feet and, 54
  turnips stuffed with, 70
Artichoke pie, 66
Artichokes, garlic sauce for, 85

Banbury cakes, 114
Banquets, Elizabethan,
  13–15
  menus for, 123–24
Barme, 125
Bastard wine, 125
Bean tart, 72
Beer, 29
Beet tart, 68
Berberries, 125
Betony, 125
Bread, 27–28
Bucks-horn, 125
Burre roots, 125

Cabbage lettice, 125
Cakes, 28
  Banbury, 114
  fine, 93
Capon in orange sauce, 50
Cardoon, 125
Carp, baked stuffed, 56
Carrots, candied, 119
Chicken
  in orange sauce, 50
  pie, 52
  prune sauce for, 84
Chicken liver pâté, 41

Coffin, 125
Comfits, 15, 125
Conneis, 125
Cookies, almond, 95
Corance, 125
Cubeb, 125
Currans, 125

Damaske water, 125
Date-spinach fritters, 74
Dining parlor, Elizabethan,
  16–22
Distilled waters, 30–31
Drinks, 17, 28–31

Eel and onion pie, 42
Egg yolks, 33–34
Erringo roots, 15, 126

Fagot, 126
Fallow deer, 126
Farms, 126
Fartes, 126
Fine cakes, 93
Fish, 20
  eel and onion pie, 42
  herring-fruit pie, 44
  stuffed, baked, 56
Fish steaks, poached, 61
Flowers, 25
  candied, 119
Fowl, 19–20
  chicken pie, 52
  goose sauce for, 83
  onion sauce for, 87
  in orange sauce, 50
  See also Chicken
Fritters, spinach-date, 74
Fruit
  candied, 119
  and herring pie, 44

Galingale, 126
Gardens, Elizabethan, 22–25
Garlic sauce, 85
Gill, 126
Gingerbread, 97
Goose sauce, 83
Grains of paradise, 126
Grose pepper, 126
Gumtragacant, 126

Haberden, 126
Herbs, 22–23
Herring-fruit pie, 44
Hippes, 126
Hundreth, 126

Jerusalem artichoke, 126
Jumbals, 95

Kidney bean tart, 72
Kitchen gardens,
        Elizabethan, 22–25
Knots, 126

Lamb
    and oyster casserole, 58
    prune sauce for, 84
Lemon-orange marmalade,
    116
Licorice, in gingerbread, 97
Licour, 126
Lights, 126
Liver
    onion sauce for, 87
    pâté, 41
Luces, 126

Malt, 28–29
March-pane, 126
Marie, 126
Marie bone, 126
Marigolds, 25
    and parsnips, in orange
        juice, 76
Marmalade, orange, 116
Meat, 19–20

Menus, Elizabethan, 123–24
Mincemeat pie, 48
Mudefishe, 126
Muske melon, 126
Muttonball soup, spicy, 38

Nutmeg, 26
    in chicken liver pâté, 41
    in mincemeat pie, 48

Olive pie, 63
Olives, 127
Onion and eel pie, 42
Onion sauce, 87
Orange marmalade, 116
Orange sauce
    fowl in, 50
    parsnips and marigolds
        in, 76
Oranges
    and apple pie, 98
    in wine sauce, 88
Oringeado, 127
Oyster and lamb casserole, 58

Pap, 127
Parsnips
    candied, 119
    and marigolds, in orange
        juice, 76
Paste, 127
Pâté, chicken liver, 41
Pear pie, 100
Pears, candied, 119
Pestell, 127
Pie pastry
    ale, 110
    rose-water, 113
    savory, 108
Pies, 20–21, 33
    apple and orange, 98
    artichoke, 66
    chicken, 52
    eel and onion, 42
    herring-fruit, 44
    mincemeat, 48
    olive, 63

pear, 100
  See also Tarts
Pigs' feet and apples, 54
Pilles, 127
Pipkin, 127
Pomewater, 127
Pompion, 127
Pork, goose sauce for, 83
Posset, 127
Pottel, 127
Prune sauce, 84
Pudding, 21–22
  chicken liver pâté, 41
  fish stuffed with, 56
  rice, 90
  turnips stuffed with, 70
Puff, 127
Pulse, 127

Q*uelquechose*
  oyster-lamb, 58
  parsnip and marigold, 76

R*aspe*, 127
Red sage, 127
Renaissance salad, 79
Rice pudding, 90
Rose water, 25, 33–34
  in almond tarts, 103
  in jumbals, 95
  in mincemeat pie, 48
  in orange and apple pie, 98
  in orange wine sauce, 88
  in pear pie, 101
  in pie pastry, 113
  in snow on an apple tree,
    120
  in spinach tarts, 104
  in suckets, 119

S*ack*, 30
Salad, Renaissance, 79
Salmon steaks, poached, 61
Sammonde, 127
Samphire, 127

Sauce
  garlic, 85
  goose, 83
  onion, 87
  orange
    fowl in, 50
    parsnips and marigolds
      in, 76
  orange wine, 88
  prune, 84
  wine, oranges in, 88
Shortbread, 93
Sippets, 127
Skirrets, 127
Snow on an apple tree, 120
Sops, 128
Soup
  muttonball, spicy, 38
  veal, 36
Spices, 26–27
Spinach-date fritters, 74
Spinach tart, 104
Strawberry leaves, in
    stuffed veal scallops, 63
Stuffe, 128
Succades, 128
Succory, 128
Suckets, 15, 119, 128
Suet, 128
Sugar, 26

T*arts*, 20–22, 33
  almond, 103
  beet, 68
  kidney bean, 72
  spinach, sweet, 104
  See also Pies
Tawney, 128
Teg, 128
Tele, 128
Tench, 128
  stuffed, baked, 56
Turnips stuffed with apples, 70

V*eal*, 20
  mincemeat pie, 48

muttonball soup, 38
scallops, stuffed, 63
soup, 36
Vegetables, 22–25
candied, 119
Verjuyce, 128
Violet leaves, in stuffed veal
scallops, 63
Voider, 128

Warden, 128
Warden pie, 100
Waumes, 128
Wine, 30
Wine sauce, oranges in, 88

NOTES ON THE ILLUSTRATIONS

The front and back covers are illustrated with engravings of Moresque designs for borders of plates by the Flemish artist Peter Firens, 1597–c.1637 (Rogers Fund, 22.41.64, and The Elisha Whittelsey Collection, The Elisha Whittelsey Fund, 56.500.62).

Reproduced on the endleaves is "The View of London Bridge from East to West," an engraving published in England in 1597 by John Norden (Harris Brisbane Dick Fund, 44.85).

The illustration on the title page is from a sixteenth-century woodcut, "Queen Elizabeth" from *Sphaera Civitatis* (Gift of Henry W. Kent, 41.44.136).

Throughout the text appear details which are taken from *A Booke of Christian Prayers*, London, 1590 (Gift of Christian A. Zabriskie, 42.32); *Li Tre Trattati*, a treatise on linen folding, stewardship, and carving techniques, by Mattia Giegher, Padua, 1639 (Harris Brisbane Dick Fund, 40.84); and *Lo Scalco alla Moderna*, a guide for stewards, by Antonio Latini, Naples, 1694 (The Elisha Whittelsey Collection, The Elisha Whittelsey Fund, 49.42.3). The dancing couples are reproduced from "German Ladies and Gentlemen Dancing," engravings by the Netherlandish artist J. T. de Bry, 1596 (The Elisha Whittelsey Collection, The Elisha Whittelsey Fund, 51.501.5788-9). The flowers which appear throughout the book are details from an engraving by the German artist Paul Flindt, 1590–1620 (Harris Brisbane Dick Fund, 37.40.5[39]).

The engraved portrait of Queen Elizabeth on page 12 was published by Paul de la Houve, probably French (Harris Brisbane Dick Fund, 17.3.756-1618). The portrait on page 123 is an engraving of Princess Elizabeth, said to be done about 1554 (Anonymous gift, 58.549.442).

Designed by Peter Oldenburg
Type set by Custom Composition Company, Inc.
Printed by Colorcraft Offset Incorporated
Bound by Sendor Bindery, Inc.

THE HARE
AND THE TORTOISE

To my sporty Lil'
Love Mum
L.K.

For Keith,
who slowly,
slowly won the day!
J.N.

ORCHARD BOOKS
338 Euston Road, London NW1 3BH
Orchard Books Australia
Level 17/207 Kent Street, Sydney, NSW 2000

First published in 2011
First paperback publication in 2012

ISBN 978 1 40830 960 5 (hardback)
ISBN 978 1 40830 968 1 (paperback)

Text © Lou Kuenzler 2011
Illustrations © Jill Newton 2011

The rights of Lou Kuenzler to be identified as the author and
Jill Newton to be identified as the illustrator of this work
has been asserted by them in accordance
with the Copyright, Designs and Patents Act, 1988.

A CIP catalogue record for this book is available
from the British Library.

1 3 5 7 9 10 8 6 4 2 (hardback)
1 3 5 7 9 10 8 6 4 2 (paperback)

Printed in Great Britain

Orchard Books is a division of Hachette Children's Books,
an Hachette UK company.